Prais

"*Driven by Purpose* is an easy-to-read book that will have you thinking about how you're planning to leave a legacy for your loved ones. It's funny, insightful, and full of concrete examples."

—*Perry Esler, Executive Director, Jesse's Journey*

"Through these stories, Ryan brings us into his world and the amazing people who have made an extraordinary impact on his life. These stories are inspiring, entertaining, and full of practical examples of how to grow your wealth and leave a transformational legacy. The people in these stories are real people, impacting real lives and motivating us to find our purpose and leave our legacy. Thank you, Ryan, for sharing these amazing people with us."

—*Susan Marshall, CEO, Brain Tumour Foundation of Canada*

"A wonderful collection of heartfelt stories on how everyday Canadians plan their estate and financial future. There is a lot of secret, hard-won wisdom here that I wish more advisors would share."

—*Paul Nazareth, Planned Giving Expert & Educator*

DRIVEN BY
Purpose

DRIVEN BY
Purpose

32 Remarkable Stories about Growing Your Wealth and Leaving a Transformational Legacy

RYAN FRASER

CFP®, CIM, MFA-P™

MILNER & ASSOCIATES INC

· EDITING · PUBLISHING · COMMUNICATIONS · CONSULTING ·

ISBN 978-1-988344-22-5 (paperback)
ISBN 978-1-988344-23-2 (e-book)

Production Credits
Editor and project manager: Karen Milner
Copy editor: Lindsay Humphreys
Interior design and typesetting: Ian Koo, DesignKoo
Cover design: Ian Koo, DesignKoo
Printer: O.J.Graphix Inc.

Published by Milner & Associates Inc.
www.milnerassociates.ca

Printed in Canada
10 9 8 7 6 5 4 3 2 1

This book is dedicated to all the amazing individuals
I have been honoured to work with in my practice and,
in particular, to those who inspired me to become
a financial planner in my early years working in the industry:
Lynn MacMillan, Denis Olivier and John MacDonald.

Most of all, this book is dedicated to our many
wonderful clients with whom we work every day —
your stories are the heart of this book.

Contents

Preface

I've been working on this book on and off for almost five years. The drive to write it came from working with the many, many wonderful clients I have met over my career as a financial planner. I knew that their experiences and the strategies we've put in place together could be helpful to many other people who are trying to plan, not only for their estate to transition to future generations, but also to broaden the reach of their legacy to help others. Most of the clients we work with want to make charitable giving and philanthropy an important part of their financial and estate planning, but they don't always know the best way to go about it.

I have known for a long time that the stories of others can be incredibly instructive and inspiring, offering us ideas and the motivation to move forward with them. There are stories I wanted to share to help others in their planning journey, but I found it challenging to put those stories into words in a way that didn't become overly dry and technical, like many books are in my field. Unless you are exceptionally weird or a working professional, reading a dry and technical book on financial and estate planning probably isn't very interesting to you.

As you read through this book, you will learn about financial and estate concepts in a practical and entertaining way, through the eyes of remarkable people. You will read stories about real folks from all walks of life — from a baker who became a millionaire, to a feisty old lady scheming to get revenge on naughty relatives who were trying to swindle her, and even a young man hit by a meteorite in his back yard.

I had actually almost completed the manuscript for this book by 2015, when my mom fell terminally ill with breast cancer. After she passed away, I realized that I had learned many small but important aspects of financial and estate planning that could only be learned in real life. With that experience in mind, I threw out nearly everything I had written and started from scratch, having realized that, as much as I talk about all of this stuff on a day-to-day basis, our experience with Mom's estate had made me a vastly better planner. As they say, when you "walk the talk," you have a very different perspective than when something is just theoretical.

As you will read in one of the later chapters, my family learned that it's not the big-picture items that bring the most stress when dealing with an estate, it's the little things. As hard as that time was for all of us, it made me a better financial planner, a better human being, and, ultimately, a better author on the topic. It is my deepest hope that what I have learned from personal experience in the last few years will help you when (not if) the time comes in your life to face similar challenges.

I owe a tremendous debt of gratitude to all the amazing people I have met and worked with over the last fifteen years. Their stories make up the heart of this book, and they are too numerous to mention. Most of the folks featured here know I have told their story, but in some cases, they have passed away. In almost every chapter, I have changed names and some details to ensure privacy. Some of the stories you will read here are an amalgamation of more than one person or situation, but every story is based on true experiences from our financial planning practice.

Another huge debt is owed to my friend, colleague, fellow author, and all-around wonderful person, Keith Thomson, and even more so to his wife, Tanja. Keith and his business partner, Serena Hak, have been patiently harassing me — well OK, not so patiently — for years, knowing I was working on this book, and occasionally calling me to the carpet for not having finished it. As persistent as Keith was (thanks, buddy!), my breakthrough came via Tanja.

I woke up one morning to a lovely email from Tanja, forwarded to me by Keith with the intriguing subject "I hate it when my wife loves you more than she loves me." Tanja had read one of my monthly newsletters and made some wonderfully kind comments about how we incorporate storytelling into our newsletters. She went on to say that she would love to read a financial book written in the same style. In that moment, I knew why I had started and restarted this book so many times — I was telling readers what to do and why, and even how, but it was just information and not storytelling. That was the missing piece that had been bugging me all those years. This book is the child of that epiphany, and for that, Tanja is going to get the first copy. (Keith will have to wait just a little bit longer, but he's had a lot of practice.)

Along with Keith, my dear friends Adam Chapman and Susan Relecom were kind enough to read through the book in its very roughest draft. Many thanks to the three of them for their insights, which helped shape the final outcome, as well as to the incredible editing skills of Karen Milner, of Milner & Associates. I've been blessed to work with Karen, who has edited so many of my favourite reads in the world of financial planning over the years.

At our firm, I work every day with some amazing colleagues who supported and encouraged me while I was writing this book: Sarah Morkin, Jane Davis, Linda Lustins, and Marian Hundt. Each has been an inspiration to me in our time together, and each has been a sounding board for various ideas and topics that are woven throughout the book.

Finally, I owe much to Denis Olivier and John MacDonald, two very fine financial planners, along with my wonderful friend and former mentor, Lynn MacMillan, who all inspired me to become a planner early in my career. While I have lost touch with Denis and John over the years, the many professional lessons they taught me in my first few years in the industry laid the groundwork for the work I do today. Lynn was, and remains, a dear friend and role model, whose time as my manager showed me what it means to manage people with compassion, skill, and knowledge. It is a rare day in my professional life when I fail to think back to conversations I had with one of these three fine people over our years working together.

I hope you enjoy reading these stories as much as I have enjoyed putting them to paper. More than this, though, I hope that when you finish this book, you will be inspired to take action on your own planning work and leave a legacy that you and your family can be proud of for generations.

Part 1

Owning Your Legacy with Style

No matter what profession you are in, there are some clients you will remember for the rest of your life. Sometimes it's because of their strong personality or a remarkable circumstance; other times, it's because of the lesson you learned through working with them, which you then incorporate in all your future work.

The extraordinary people you are about to meet in Part 1 can teach us all how to embrace life, how to make an impact, and how to take charge of our own legacy. Every day their stories inspire me, and I hope they will inspire you as well.

1

The Man Who Won It All, and Then Gave It All Away

One of the joys of living in Canada is that we get to help fund our government by making voluntary donations.[1] Everyone's favourite voluntary donation is to the government-run lotteries, such as Lotto 649 and Lotto Max. In honour of a recent large lottery win here in London, Ontario, I want to tell you about the man who won it all — and gave it all away.

When I met Sammy, he was in his late sixties. Sammy had an amazing life story. He had been born in desperate conditions in a third-world country run by a dictator, ravaged by war and violence. It was, as one might imagine, not a great place to grow up. The village in which he was raised had neither a sewer system nor running water. It was impossible to build basic infrastructure in a place where war was a constant threat.

---

1   Most of the time, this is called "tax" and it's a three-letter swear word.

Determined to find a better life by the time he was twenty, Sammy hid aboard a cargo ship in order to escape. It seemed to him better to risk being lost at sea than to stay where he was. Eventually that ship found its way to Halifax, and he arrived in Canada as a refugee. Sammy built a life for himself here; he married, settled down, and started a family with his wife, Mary. Every day, he would say, was like winning the lottery. That proved to be an apt turn of phrase because, one day, Sammy did in fact win the lottery and suddenly found himself a millionaire.

Can you imagine what it would be like, coming from such humble beginnings, grateful for every day you wake up in freedom, to find yourself wealthy in an instant? What do you think you would do? The stats say that most lotto winners end up blowing it all, often in a matter of a few years.

Well, Sammy's decision was to give almost all of it away. Some went to his church, as a thank you for the support he had received from that community on his arrival in Canada as a desperate young man fleeing violence. Some went to family. The bulk of it, however, went back to his home country, to the village he grew up in, where he helped pay for the installation of sewer infrastructure. It was an unglamorous, but desperately needed, gift. Here in Canada we would take something like this for granted, but Sammy knew that this was fundamental to the well-being of everyone in the village: the generous gift of sanitation, cleanliness, and health. I suppose you could say that most lotto winnings go down the toilet, but in this case, Sammy's lotto winnings actually allowed people to *have* a toilet!

When he returned to Canada, Sammy took the last remaining lottery funds and used them as collateral for a business loan a friend needed. A year later, the business failed, and the bank foreclosed on the loan. Despite everything, it never bothered Sammy that he had had so much money and now it was all gone. Instead, what kept him up at night was how he was treated, both with and without the money.

"Ryan," he told me once in tears, "that money was never mine. God lent it to me to do good in the world, and we did that, and I am proud of it and have no regrets. But I can't get over how the bank treated me like a god the day we won the money, but then treated us like dirt when they took the last of it away. I'll never forget that feeling until my dying day."

He never did get over that feeling, and that was how we started working together. Understandably, he no longer wanted to deal with the bank, and instead he chose to work with me over the last few years of his life. I was so very grateful to have the chance to spend some time with Sammy and Mary. They were wonderful people, with such a great grasp on the important things in life. A couple of years after we met, Sammy died at a far-too-young age, as his early life had taken a heavy toll on his long-term health.

His was a life very well-lived, indeed. He passed away many years ago, and I still think of him fondly, as I am sure do many others.[2] Early in my career as a planner, Sammy's story and the

---

2   In a tribute to his kindness, generosity, and impact on the world around him, nearly 750 of us showed up for his funeral, in a church designed to hold only 500. All this for a man who had only a handful of family members in Canada!

deep respect so many who knew him had for him, served as a strong lesson to me that money is only a tool, and it is our intent and how we use it that will define us forever. Sammy could have taken his winnings and spent them on himself; instead, he looked at the world around him, saw what needed doing, and invested in the people he loved. We live in a society where these basic truths are often overlooked and forgotten. Our fulfillment and happiness should be measured by the quality of our lives — not the quantity of wealth we hold.

Anna, the Ultimate Secret Santa

I've been waiting to tell this story for almost two decades, about the nicest, sweetest client I have ever known, who had me incorporate a very special revenge in her financial plan. She has long since passed away, but her story shows us that revenge can be motivated by kindness and hard-won life lessons, not just malice.

Early on in my career, I met an amazing lady, who we'll call Anna. She was already well into her eighties at that point, and I worked with her for a number of years as her financial planner. Anna was a delight to work with — bright, articulate, very informed, and opinionated. She was also worth a whole heck of a lot of money.

Anna, like many seniors, was very concerned about spending her money, as she was worried she might run out. In her late eighties, she was in great shape and planned to live a long time. That probably doesn't surprise you, but what might surprise you is why she was so focused on her longevity. Anna planned to live a long time because she wanted to tick off "the greedy little buggers" (her words, not mine).

You see, Anna was worth nearly $10 million. She was a testament to a lifetime of chronic saving, and she had invested over the years in a wide variety of things. But the main source of growth in her wealth had been real estate. She had been hanging on to some properties for a very long time.

Anna had some very greedy descendants who had a good suspicion of just how much she was worth. They would try any number of tactics to swindle her out of her money. She had seen everything, from them trying to get her to sign deeds of properties over to them, to being told elaborate tales about why someone needed large sums of money in a hurry.

Being a sharp, strategic, and crafty gal, Anna's ultimate plan was to outlive most of her scheming heirs. But, just in case, she asked me to do some very creative planning work to minimize what they would get out of her estate and to ensure that her more generous plans for her wealth were met. And boy, did we ever have fun!

Making Private Transactions by Bypassing the Estate

Anna had one niece (we'll call her Josie) who had always been kind to her and had no idea of Anna's net worth. Anna's main goal was to make sure that Josie was taken care of properly. Her other planning goal was to ensure that the Greedy Little Buggers (GLBs) got what they wanted, but in the most inconvenient way. All of this, of course, was the backup plan to Anna's master plan of outliving her greedy family members.

After some research, and coordination with Anna's lawyer, we determined our best way forward was to move Anna's cash holdings into the insurance-company version of GICs (which go by many different names, such as Guaranteed Interest Options, Accumulation Annuities, and others), as well as into Segregated Funds. Both of these options come with a named beneficiary, which meant for Anna that she could have the funds completely bypass her estate and go directly to Josie. Unlike a will, which may be a public document, the insurance beneficiary designation is usually a private transaction and, in most provinces, not subject to public knowledge or scrutiny. This allowed Anna to pass her cash quietly on to Josie, and leave the part of the estate covered by her will solely to the GLBs; without the cash, that portion consisted of little more than her extensive real estate holdings, which would incur very significant capital gains tax consequences at the time of her death.

How We Created a Cash Crunch in Anna's Estate

With the majority of her estate subject to capital gains, and most of the cash re-directed to Josie via insurance, Anna's plan was to name all the GLBs as joint executors, stipulating in her will that they must all be in 100 percent agreement in order to sign off on any distributions. In her opinion, the most likely outcome was that they would bicker and argue with one another. They would ultimately have to sell or mortgage many of the properties they so badly wanted to inherit, just to pay the tax bill due on her death, and it would take a long time for the estate to settle. And Anna was just fine with that — the one and only time I have had a client who actually wanted to drag out her estate's settlement period! As many of the GLBs were already in their sixties and seventies, she was hoping that by the time they received their "just due," they wouldn't be in any shape to enjoy the fruits of their many years of scheming.

Anna's plan was driven by her love and appreciation for Josie and she wanted to reward her niece's kindness and generosity with her own, in the form of the quiet legacy that she would ensure was left to her wonderfully kind niece. Unfortunately, it's not uncommon for people who have built significant wealth to feel that they are the targets of less-well-off relatives who have ulterior motives and their own personal plans for that money. Anna's estate plan can be a valuable lesson for anyone who wants to keep their legacy away from the grabbing hands of their own GLBs and guarantee that as much as possible is left to the people or causes they value.

The Ultimate Realization of Anna's Plan

Anna lived a long life, long enough to celebrate her one-hundredth birthday in full control of her faculties. Unfortunately, I didn't get to remain her advisor as I took a promotion a few years after we structured her holdings and I had to pass her accounts on to a colleague. However, my colleague did let me know several years later when Anna passed away that she had outlived two-thirds of the GLBs, and that Josie had been stunned to receive a quiet but very significant inheritance although she had expected and wanted nothing at all from her aunt.

As for me, I'm always going to remember with great fondness a very kind, sweet, insanely smart, and funny lady who took the time to knit my newborn son a sweater. Anna was one of those special clients who taught me so much while I was advising her over the years; her creative estate plan was one of the ways in which she reminded me of the truly important things in life — that sometimes karma is sweeter than honey.

3

The
Wisdom of
Stella

One of my favourite quotes, attributed to a variety of sources, is, "Fish and family both go bad after three days." I love that saying. Mind you, I love my family too, but I think we can all admit that family dynamics have their ups and downs. The fish quote somehow captures the complexity of those dynamics in such a wonderful way.

A client of mine, Stella, turned eighty a few years ago, sold her home, and needed to make some changes to her finances in order to transition to renting. Her kids were all actively helping her out in different ways — after fifty years in the same house, moving is a big, big deal. The kids all loved their mom and were all working hard to make sure that she made the best decisions for herself and that the move went as smoothly as possible. In their eyes, they really wanted to make sure she understood what she was doing.

If I have learned anything in my career, it's that the smartest people in the world are octogenarian ladies.[3] You might disagree, but having had a few behind-the-scenes conversations with several of them over the years, I can tell you with pretty good certainty, these ladies are sharp. Way sharper than anyone gives them credit for. If you don't believe me, re-read the previous chapter about Anna, the ultimate Secret Santa. Trust me, these gals have a gift.

Stella was really good at "playing dumb" in public with her kids. In almost every aspect of life, she'd ask them for help and advice, and get their opinions on what course of action they felt she should take. Each of her children got a say in what was going on, and Stella would factor all of that into her planning and decision making. When it came time for us to work on her financial plans together, her kids would be involved in some of the meetings and she would ask me to outline everything I had earlier suggested to her to each of them. I'd patiently answer their questions — sometimes multiple times to each of the children separately if a family meeting wasn't possible.

When it came time to make the actual changes to her financial and estate plans, though, I had to ask all the kids to leave the room. One thing we learn as financial planners is that when significant changes are made to a client's financial goals in later years, it is very important to ensure that you can make a strong case, if need be, that there was no undue influence when so many family members have been part of the action. Given the relatively large family

---

3   They have told me this, and I utterly believe them.

Stella had, this was a crucial step. Not all the kids were happy with this part of the process, but we had laid out the plan to the entire family, so everyone was willing to "back off" to let us chat alone, even if some were reluctant to do so.

When the door closed and it was just Stella and I, she dropped the bewildered and confused old lady act she had been putting on. Suddenly, there she was, sharp as a tack. "OK, now listen up," she would say to me. "Here's what is going to happen." Stella then would spend five minutes outlining to me the exact family dynamic between her kids. She wanted me to take notes: what her concerns were, how each of her kids might react to different decisions she was making, and what the family dynamic would be after she passed away. After that, we would sign all the necessary paperwork, and the direction for her future was set.

Man, that lady was *smart*. Her insights and predictions were like a crystal ball reading. Pretty much everything she outlined to me came true exactly as she had described, down to the smallest detail of how her children would respond to her and each other. I looked back at my notes years later, after she passed way, and sure enough, she had called the family dynamics perfectly. Everything she had done in her estate and financial plans in those later years executed perfectly, just as she intended — and in many cases, her intentions were to preserve and heal the family dynamics of her children. It was a beautiful thing to watch her plans execute so flawlessly.

The moral of this story (other than never underestimate an octogenarian lady!) is that you should never, ever, underestimate the knowledge that experience brings. In our First Nations communities, elders are valued in a way that Western culture does not fully appreciate. Stella was such a huge example to me of why we should honour the wisdom of our elders more often.

One last cute story about Stella, who never failed to make me laugh: Part of her planning involved setting up a life annuity to fund her living expenses as long as she lived. The cheque to pay for it was the largest cheque of her life, and her hand actually trembled as she wrote it. She told me it was the biggest cheque she had ever written and that she nearly died of a heart attack right there when she signed.

In a coincidence, the annuity went into effect just a few days before her birthday, and thus began an annual ritual of her calling me a few days before each birthday. Each year, I received a call from her, asking me when the annuity would run out. I said, "Never, it will last as long as you do." She said thanks and hung up. The next year, I got the same call, as I did every year after that.

Stella finally admitted to me around year five that she only called to rub it in to the insurance company that she was still around, and they had to pay her forever. She just really liked the sound of my voice confirming she was still around to collect that year's payment. We did that every year until the day she died, and it was a highlight of the year for both of us.

Such a wonderful lady — I'll remember Stella when I'm in my eighties, making the same call to my advisor. She taught me the importance of always looking closely at family dynamics when doing any kind of estate or financial planning. You can have a perfect plan on paper, but if a family member were to take issue with any planning, the entire plan can quickly go down the drain. Stella's understanding of her large family meant that the bequeathing of her estate went as smoothly as possible, and everyone felt appreciated and involved. Her biggest wish — family harmony — came true due to her strong maternal instincts and insights.

4

Keeping the Lights On, Instead of Putting Your Name in Lights

I f you have ever been involved in founding a charity or have "worked on the inside," you gain a new perspective on the vital importance of donations to help support operational funding. My thoughts again turned to this topic recently when I had the honour of attending the funeral of Julia Wagg, who, with her wife Holly, founded the Ten Oaks Project (www.tenoaksproject.org) in Ottawa over a decade ago. Julia died of leukemia just a few days before her thirty-seventh birthday.

Her memorial service was extremely moving, as she had touched so many people in her brief but significant time with us.[4]

---

4   It was also perhaps the first memorial service in history to include the camp song "Baby Shark," which Julia was famous for leading at Ten Oaks!

For me, one of the most poignant moments involved her "parting charitable gift" to the Ten Oaks Project, the Wagg Legacy Fund. Julia and Holly had created a fund specifically to provide long-term stability and operational funding to the organization they founded, and their friends, family, and colleagues were asked to commit to monthly donations to the fund in Julia's memory to provide a lasting legacy that will ensure organizational stability. Their gift isn't "sexy," but it is ever so significant.

Where Your Money Goes When You Donate

When I work with clients on planning charitable gifts from their estate, one of the most common questions I get is centered around how effectively charities spend their money, and how much of the gift ends up going to administration costs. It's a natural question for people to ask; after all, they worked hard for the money they are giving away and want to know that it is being used responsibly and for maximum impact. But there is a lot of background needed to answer the question properly.[5]

In my experience, most people are surprised to learn that the vast majority of charitable organizations actually have administration and salary costs that are too *low* relative to the work they are doing. In particular, small to medium-sized organizations are

---

5   If you know someone who works at a charity and you really don't like them, bring this up as a topic of conversation. I guarantee you it will drive them absolutely insane faster than anything else you could do.

often understaffed and perform an incredible amount of work relative to the dollars raised and spent. The reasons are complex, but one of the root causes is that funders and donors are often reluctant to fund the day-to-day operations of a charity. It is much more "sexy" to donate to specific causes or to fund specific projects (research, for example) than it is to fund the more basic things like keeping the lights on and paying staff.

As someone who has helped found a charity, I can't begin to tell you the frustration of trying to find creative ways to run an organization when finding operational funding[6] to support it is very, very difficult.[7] The net result is that many charitable organizations do not have the long-term stability necessary to execute effectively on their mission. Since organizational funding is not stable into the future, many staff members in the not-for-profit sector work on short-term contracts of less than two years and have relatively low job security. As a result, the industry as a whole understandably sees a lot of turnover.

In my experience, employees in not-for-profits work for about 70 percent of the salary of an equivalent for-profit position, and in most cases have limited or poor benefits. Yet these very same people, driven by their passion for the mission and mandate of

---

6   Operational funding is a very specific term in the charity world. It is unrestricted money that that can be used by the organization to run its general operations, and is not tied to any specific project. Much of the time, charity funding is classed as restricted funding (i.e., tied to a specific project or purpose) and often cannot be used to run the charity's basic operations.

7   Operational funding is notoriously difficult to find, which makes anyone willing to donate to this cause a hero to the board and staff of any charity.

their organization, often work harder and for longer hours than their for-profit equivalents. Job stress can be very, very high, as organizational resources are extremely limited. In many cases, one full-time worker in a charity does the job of two or three people in the private sector.

Don't ever doubt that if any part of your donation goes to administration, the money isn't being well spent — charities, of all organizations, know how to stretch a dollar to the limit.

Be a Julia

To me, Julia's final gift speaks to the heart of creating a quiet legacy. There are lots of people who want their name in lights, but not nearly enough people who want their gift to go toward keeping the lights on. The true heroes, in my opinion, are the people who help an organization thrive for the long term. Julia was certainly that kind of hero.

Julia's final note on LinkedIn expresses some remarkable thoughts as she approached the last weeks of her life. She so eloquently and passionately wrote about living life with significance, and her words are well worth reading. I guarantee reading it will change how you live your life. You can find Julia's final note at www.linkedin.com/pulse/i-am-going-die-julia-wagg-chrl.

5

The
Bonds
of Family

Joe and Mary, a wonderful couple nearing retirement, were referred to us by a close friend of theirs who is one of our clients. Both Mary and Joe had been diagnosed with incurable cancers and were getting their affairs in order under very difficult circumstances. Extremely warm and generous people, their family and their faith are two of the biggest anchors in their lives.

Working through their financial plan was one of the most emotional but highly rewarding moments of my entire professional career. Mary, Joe, and I had many deep and meaningful conversations about their personal legacy and values and how we might reflect them in their planning.

Mary and Joe's children are all in their early twenties and have moved across the country. One of the key legacies we identified was that they wanted to ensure their kids would remain as tight and connected long after their parents' passing as they are today. To accomplish this goal, Mary and Joe had initially thought about providing a testamentary trust within their will that would pay to bring the kids together once a year. The challenge, however, was that this would keep the estate open for many years, the trust would be subject to a high level of taxation and accounting fees, and, ultimately, it would probably not be practical. We decided instead to use legacy planning and charitable giving to tie the bonds of family together.

An Abundance of Giving

Knowing the spiritual importance of giving to Mary and Joe, I connected them to Abundance Canada, a public foundation serving a wide mandate, but with roots as a faith-based organization. Abundance Canada's strong faith-based expertise was a natural fit for Joe and Mary. Like many other community foundations, Abundance Canada offers donor-advised funds, where the foundation handles charitable receipting and then disburses funds to a variety of charities on the advice of their donors. In addition to accepting gifts immediately, they are structured to receive gifts from the donor's estate and disburse to the donor's chosen charities over time (even over many years or decades) if the donor wishes. Most importantly, the original donor can appoint a successor advisor, which in Mary and Joe's case will be the children.

For the two of them, this meant that we could do some smart tax planning now, as well as provide an opportunity for their children to get together yearly in the future to make decisions about which charities their parents' generous ongoing gifts will support. It was important to Joe and Mary that they pass on their values as well as their money, and setting their charitable giving up in this way means that not only will their kids have a reason to see each other and connect annually, but they will also be as involved in administering the family legacy as their parents were.

In the immediate term, Joe was able to make a large gift of stock (which had a significant capital gain) in-kind through Abundance Canada in lieu of his normal tithe to his church. From a tax-planning perspective, this allowed him to use the donation credit on his 2018 tax return, as he'll have little taxable employment income in 2019 after starting his disability claim late last fall. Additionally, his in-kind gift meant that he was not required to pay capital gains tax on the donated stock, and he still received a tax receipt for the entirety of his donation. Abundance Canada then disbursed the funds to the church, replacing Joe's monthly donation for the remainder of the year.

Over the next few years, Mary and Joe will continue to give to charity through their fund at Abundance Canada and start to involve the children in the decision on which organizations are supported each year. Upon their passing, a significant amount of their estate will be donated to the fund to create a legacy well beyond their lifetime. Our hope is that this family tradition of giving will continue on to the next generation and be another layer of glue in their strong family bond that will last long past Mom and Dad's lifetimes. There will always be a warm, positive reason for the four siblings to come together each year to celebrate and continue the family legacy. I think it's a beautiful, creative, positive, and elegant solution to a challenging situation, and I'm proud to have been a part of it.

Joe and Mary have had unfortunate circumstances thrust upon them, which have forced them to think about their legacy at a much younger age than most people. I deeply admire them for their courage, resilience, and warmth; they inspire me daily. Sometimes the hardest of circumstances help us to understand what's most important to us. I think that these amazing people should be an inspiration to everyone to start thinking about what your legacy will be, today.

I hope you will never find yourself in the same position that Joe and Mary have found themselves in, with a very limited time period to act on your own legacy, or at such a young age. But if you do, wouldn't you be grateful to have taken the time to think through the legacy you wish to leave to your own family?

6

Two Veterans
Who Gave Birth
to a Museum

Each November, Remembrance Day holds a special place in my heart, as I'm one of the founders of a very special charity, The Secrets of Radar Museum. During World War II, over six thousand Canadians were recruited from all walks of life and put to work on a project more secret than the search for the atomic bomb. The recruits were sent all around the world and couldn't talk about their experiences until the Official Secrets Act was lifted in 1991. It's an incredible story, as is the tale of founding the museum.

Getting Hitched to a Museum

In the late 1990s, my wife, Bridget, and I were living across the hall from one another in an apartment building on Proudfoot

Lane here in London. Our landlord was . . . interesting, to say the least. A few of us in the building got together to form a tenants-rights group to keep things in check. One of those folks was Fred Bates, who, along with his wife Jan, were both World War II radar veterans.

Fred and I hit it off right away; we were kindred spirits and not afraid to take on our landlord. As we got to know Fred and Jan, they learned that we were planning to honeymoon on the east coast and visit a pile of regional museums and heritage sites. Upon hearing this, Fred shared with us photographs and documentation from his and Jan's experiences during World War II.

Fred and Jan had met on the White Cliffs of Dover, where they were both working on a type of radar station called Oboe. Jan was the ranking women's officer — most of the stations in the UK were "womened" rather than manned — and Fred was the ranking men's officer. Everything was top secret, so you weren't allowed to talk to anyone about your work or fraternize outside your rank. As you can imagine, the two of them spent a lot of time together, which led to their marriage shortly after the war.

In the late 1990s, several World War II vets had put together a small museum in Clinton, Ontario, where many had been trained during the war. However, the museum was closed down due to some interesting financial issues. Fred found out that the materials he and Jan had donated were being stored in an unsafe environment. Fred was pretty upset; much of his memorabilia should never have existed at all post-war due to the Official Secrets Act, and now his personal record of history might be destroyed due to carelessness.

So, Fred rounded up six of us to form The Secrets of Radar Museum. I took on the role of chair and led the museum through its first six years. Fred was a force of nature, and we could certainly understand how he had risen through the ranks during the war. He was simply incapable of taking no for an answer, as many of us learned, much to our chagrin.

One night, John (our vice-chair) and I were tasked by Fred with moving a couch that had been donated to give our veterans a place to sit down at the museum. One of Fred's neighbours had given it to the museum on the condition that we retrieve it from her apartment. We found a five-dollar bill tucked in the cushions as we loaded it into the truck. We joked that we should have Fred return it instead of us, because he would be likely to come back with the dining room suite, as well as the lady's husband! Fred was just that persuasive. We wondered how we had been suckered into this whole affair — and realized it was, of course, thanks to Fred. We shared a good laugh, returned the five dollars and chuckled all the way to the museum.

Our museum was a labour of love, and a race against time. Our vets were all in their eighties and, unfortunately, we lost a few every year. We incorporated in 2001 and managed to get the doors open by 2003. We had taken what was an idea in Fred's head, and made it real. At times we wondered if it had been worth all the work, but then special moments of magic would happen.

Once, we helped a vet with Alzheimer's track down his war records to get him into the Veterans Care Program at the Parkwood Institute in London, Ontario, which provides complex continuing and long-term care for Canadian veterans. Another time, we helped four children of a deceased veteran learn where their father had been during the war, and what he had worked on. He had died just before the oath of secrecy was lifted and had never been able to tell them himself about his important contribution to the war effort. We were honoured to be his voice long after his passing.

Running a museum was not without its bumps. Working with an initial budget of just $6,000 a year, we survived on volunteer labour until we had raised enough to hire a full-time manager-curator, and we moved into an old lab in the Westminster Ponds area of London, which originally had been a veteran rehabilitation centre.

In one of those "had I known" life lessons, Jan Bates and I spent long hours working as a team, cleaning the floors and walls of the museum's new (well, not-so-new) home. Jan was quite short, so she scrubbed the floors and lower walls while I scrubbed the top half of the walls and cleaned ceiling tiles. Years later, a visitor who had worked in the lab came in, viewed a room Jan and I had scrubbed for hours and said, "Wow, how on earth did you get the goat's blood off the floor and wall there?" Jan and I shared a good laugh and agreed that we might skip lunch that day.

I could probably write another entire book on what it took to get the museum running. Operating a charity is a daunting and difficult task. It's also one of the most rewarding experiences of my life.

As much as you might think that a place like this receives a pile of government support, the museum, like so many other not-for-profit and charitable organizations, relies primarily on private donations for its survival. Never forget how important your donation is to the future of a charity. Not-for-profit organizations have to work awfully hard just to keep the lights on, and for most of them there's no "magic bullet" that pays the bills. Even organizations with government funding live a precarious existence. Your support, both in the long and short term, is crucial.

Although I have not been involved in the museum for over ten years, I'm pleased to say that, despite financial challenges at the time of writing this, our little museum is still running. It has gone through some ups and downs over the last two decades and now exists attached to the 427 (London) Wing on Crumlin Sideroad in London, Ontario. Fred and Jan have long since passed away, as have so many of my friends who were our radar veterans. I suspect that in the long term, the museum may become a virtual museum or be absorbed into a larger organization and, as a founder, I am content to see either of those things happen. We started an organization that accomplished its most important goal: to let the long-silent voices of our radar veterans be heard and to provide a therapeutic setting for them in their later years.

I, for one, will never forget them. Fred and Jan's legacy has touched so many of us. Together, we accomplished so many important things that we could never have foreseen, and touched many, many veterans and their families in the process. Never, ever forget that the organizations you support thrive only because of people like you — and the legacy you choose to leave for future generations by donating your money, time, and expertise. I hope Jan and Fred's story will inspire you to make your dreams a legacy for others, just as it did for so many of us.

Part 2

Protecting
Your
Legacy

Hopefully you've been inspired by the many stories of amazing people in the first part of this book, and you are thinking about your own legacy. In Part 2, we will take a look at some of the practical steps you can take today to ensure that the plans you make for your future, for your estate, and for the next generation will all unfold as you intend them to . . . even if life doesn't always go as expected.

7

How the Queen and Prince Left Their Kingdoms in Shambles

Once upon a time, there was a very talented, but nameless, prince. He built a fabulous empire filled with creativity, raspberry berets, song, and dance, and it was worth a fortune. A $260-million fortune, to be precise.

And the queen — oh, the queen, how well she could sing! The queen was a natural woman who was filled with soul, and she gave generously to improve civil rights, to her church, and to bring music to the people. She had R-E-S-P-E-C-T from everyone. In the end, even after her lifetime of generosity, her empire was worth $90 million.

While their music has now fallen silent, their respective kingdoms are filled with noise and strife, and much warfare. And do you know why? Neither the queen nor the prince had made plans for succession. They both died without a will.

As you have probably guessed, the Queen (of Soul) in our oh-so-true fairy tale is Aretha Franklin, who died in August 2018. And the prince is, of course, Prince (or, for a while, the artist formerly known as Prince). Legally known as Prince Robert Nelson, he was one of the most creative songwriters in modern pop history and a well-loved performer. The battle for Prince's estate is already a thing of legend; since he died in 2016, no less than forty-five people have come forward to demand a piece of the kingdom. Only time will tell how messy things will be for Aretha Franklin's estate, but at the moment, things don't bode much better in her case.

Both were phenomenal artists, the best in their fields, something that that was cleverly illustrated by one of my favourite cartoons in the weeks after Aretha Franklin's death. It showed the Queen of Soul being welcomed to the Pearly Gates by other pre-deceased musical royalty: Elvis (the King), Michael Jackson (the Prince of Pop), Prince, Duke Ellington, and Count Basie. It was a touching and brilliant tribute, one that especially resonated with me as a former professional musician.[8]

Intestacy Sucks

Aside from being phenomenal musicians, both Aretha Franklin and Prince shared a major failure: they died without a will or, in legal terms, they "died intestate." As a result, much grief and battling

---

8   My mother and her best friend hung out with Duke Ellington in the '60s and *had no idea who he was*. As a saxophone player in my first career, I was aghast that my mom had no clue she had been in the presence of musical royalty!

are still occurring over their respective estates. What eventually happens to their estates will be determined by the intestacy laws where they died, as well as by where they held property. As you can imagine, this makes things complicated and likely means that at least some of their vast wealth will not go where they would have wanted it to.

Here in Ontario, if you die without a will, the Office of the Public Guardian and Trustee (OPGT) of the Province of Ontario will represent your estate — whether you had $10 to your name, or $100 million. Relatives may petition to take over as estate trustee, but they can only do so on the authority given by the OPGT. No matter what, if you die without a will, your estate will be distributed by a formula, and it is not likely to be the formula you would have used.[9]

Things can get even messier, though, if you own assets in different jurisdictions: it's possible your estate can be subject to other provinces' (or countries'!) rules as well. Needless to say, costs (and family grief) can add up quickly.

An Old Will Is Problematic, Too

I can't emphasize enough how important it is to update your will. One of the most important things to know is that, in Ontario, your will is invalidated upon marriage — but *not* upon separation or divorce.

9　You can find the Ontario formula here:
　www.attorneygeneral.jus.gov.on.ca/english/family/pgt/heirclaim.php

Even if your marriage situation is stable, it's quite likely you've had major changes in your life over the last five years. If so, pull out your will, dust it off, and revise it if necessary. And remember, being an executor or estate trustee is a *big* job — make sure the person you originally named is still up to it, and try to have multiple backups. You can't know for certain that the person you named will be willing or able when the time comes.

And please, please, *please*, get a qualified estate lawyer to draft your will. It's worth spending a tiny bit more to ensure your estate is not tied up because of legal issues that will also drive costs up in the long run. I once worked with a family where a badly worded will resulted in more than $125,000 in legal fees, all of which had to be paid from the estate — effectively leaving the beneficiaries with nothing. An estate specialist can anticipate many problems that non-specialists would not think to address in your situation.

Remember to Support Your Favourite Causes

More than 80 percent of us donate to charity in our lifetime — but only 4 percent do so at death through a charitable gift in our will. From a tax-planning scenario, arranging to give at death is often hugely effective. I always like to say that you can give to three places at death: family, charity, and tax. Pick any two you like.

Remember the Tale of the Queen and Prince

So, give your heirs some Respect. Say a Little Prayer and this Manic Monday, put on your Raspberry Beret and go see your lawyer. I Feel for You in wanting to procrastinate, but Nothing Compares 2 U when you break the Chain of Fools so that When Doves Cry, there will be no Controversy for your empire.[10]

There is no time like now (or when you are done this book) to give your lawyer a call, get your will up to date, and then put on a few of these great tunes to celebrate the lives of these two remarkable musicians.

---

10 I have at least two more paragraphs of song titles I want to end with, but U Got the Look that you will go Daydreaming if I continue.

8

Pirates, Ghosts, and Life Insurance

As we've discussed a number of times, most likely it's going to suck to be dead. And while you can't do much other than defer that reality, fortunately, there's a lot you can do to mitigate the financial effects.[11]

The original concept of life insurance largely predates modern society's concept of it. As early as 5,000 BC, sailors in China came up with the idea of protecting one another from pirates at sea by using shared risk for their cargo. The idea was, if pirates slaughtered a ship's crew for its cargo, at least some of the assets being shipped would make it to port via another vessel. Good for

---

11 Not for you, yourself, mind you. You're not going to need money where you're going.

the business, but maybe not so much for the family of the poor sailors. We need to go forward another five millennia to find a more evolved example of life insurance that leaves the surviving family members in a better place.

The Burial Club . . . for Military Men

The modern concept of life insurance seems to date back to about 100 BC, in Rome. Gaius Marius created a "burial club" for his troops, in which everyone pitched in to pay for the funeral costs of fellow troops and provide a stipend to surviving family. This plan was driven by a concern that Romans not buried with proper funeral rites would come back as ghosts and angrily haunt their friends and family.

It probably wasn't hard to get the troops to buy in to this plan. We've all worked with someone we really, definitely don't want to be working with for eternity. Still, I don't know about you, but I for one am glad that workplace clubs have gotten a bit more positive in nature over the last two millennia!

Life Insurance Today

Although rules around insurance have changed a lot in the last two thousand–plus years, the basic concept has remained: you die, and someone else gets money. Here in Canada, the key piece of this is that the government treats inheriting insurance money as a tax-free payout, hence the power and purpose of using life insurance for planning your estate. If you stop to think about it, relatively few assets are subject to zero tax in Canada: your principal residence, your tax-free savings account (TFSA) — and that, quite frankly, is about it. Everything else you might own has some kind of tax consequence. Fortunately, there are several neat and interesting options for using life insurance to minimize the tax impact of most kinds of investments on your estate and to help you accomplish many of your other financial goals.[12]

Replacement of Lost Income

There is absolutely no way to know how much money you'll have when the Grim Reaper comes knock-knock-knockin' at your door. While you may have plenty of money today, you might not have any when the doorbell-of-doom rings and a guy with a cowl and scythe comes looking for you. But there is a way to guarantee that you will have assets to pass on to your beneficiaries. Purchasing insurance will ensure (See what I did there?) that your family has funds no matter what.

As much as we first think of life insurance being used to help cover funeral costs and the tax bill that's due upon death, its most important purpose is to provide income for your beneficiaries that would otherwise be lost when they lose you. This is particularly important for families in which there are young dependants, or in situations where you're providing for someone else. It's especially

12   Still, it sucks to be dead. I suppose that goes without saying.

important if you have a family member with a special need or disability, and funds absolutely *must* be in place for their protection after you are gone.

It's the Cheapest Way to Pay Tax

We often set up life insurance policies to pay the taxes that come due on the death of the second spouse. These taxes can be a very significant cost to your estate and will reduce the amount you can leave to your beneficiaries. In many cases, especially the younger you start, the insurance may be a lower cost-per-dollar to cover tax costs than actually paying the eventual tax bill itself.

These taxes most often arise from the assets in your RRSP, RRIF, defined-contribution pension plan, or taxable capital gains (from investments, secondary properties, business assets, etc.), all of which get added to your income in your year of death. For many people, this can be a very substantial amount of money.

For a rough calculation of the potential impact to your estate, add up all of your money that's in registered accounts (such as RRIFs, RRSPs, and defined-contribution pensions), as well as one-half of the capital gains on your non-registered investments. Now, divide that total in half. Your result will give you a pretty close approximation of the worst-case tax owing on your estate in most provinces. (You can take this strategy a step further and use the insurance proceeds as a charitable gift to lessen the tax impact even more, but that's a subject for a whole other day, or at least chapters 26 and 32.)

Tax-efficient Strategy for Business Owners

If you own a private corporation that holds significant passive investment assets, life insurance can be an extremely tax-efficient way to transfer funds out of your company through your estate, tax-free to beneficiaries. Under the current small-business rules, the insurance grows tax-free in your corporation and eventually will pay out tax-free via your capital dividend account. This strategy also helps to avoid some double-taxation traps on transfers of private companies.

While recent federal tax proposals might end up having an effect on this, from what we know, the strategy described above appears to remain a valid and viable planning strategy at the moment and not affected by the proposed changes to date. However, it is entirely possible that, by the time you are reading this, the rules will have changed; so, be sure to consult with your accountant before implementing any insurance strategies in your corporation!

One *immensely* important thing: Generally, the beneficiary of your corporate-owned insurance policies should *almost always* be the corporation, not your family or any other beneficiary. If you don't follow this rule, the tax consequences can be very, very severe.

Choosing the Right Type of Insurance

There's a whole pile of different types of insurance you can buy, but for most estate-planning purposes, it's important to choose something that will last as long as you do. This usually means one of three policy options: universal life, whole life, or term-to-100.

Most importantly, it means you should work with someone who really understands how these policies work and vary, because it is often misleading for the average person to compare the policies (and the insurance companies that offer them) solely on premium price and projections of future values, as the company-produced illustrations are based on certain assumptions that may vary widely across companies.[13] A competent, trained specialist can help you sort through the otherwise mind-numbing features and benefits available, and the pros and cons of each, in light of your own circumstances.

For most of us, life insurance is not a whole lot of fun to think about, but it sure can make a big impact on your estate planning. We've come a long way from pirates and burial clubs, but at the end of the day, doing it "right and boring" with insurance makes a lot of sense for most estates.

Gaius Marius started something incredible nearly two thousand years ago, and it can — and likely should — be a major part of your own estate plans. Make sure you take a look at your situation and determine if life insurance is a good idea for you too.

---

13 Unfortunately, there is no standard in the insurance industry for assumptions used in illustrations and, therefore, illustrations are based on a number of assumptions. As a consumer, this makes it *exceedingly* difficult to do a true comparison between options based on illustrations alone. Historically, insurers have often done some "creative marketing" to make their product look better in comparison to the competition. The only values that you can rely on to make a decision in an illustration 100 percent of the time are "guaranteed" values. Even this does not give you the full picture.

9

Would You
Let a Brain Surgeon
Fix Your Car?

I'm a ridiculously loyal client when I find great service. I've had the same hairdresser, Octavia, for twenty-two years. When I started going, I wanted Octavia to dye my hair grey, because I had just started teaching at Western University and someone had mistaken me for a first-year student in the men's room. Now, she likes to point out that the grey has taken hold naturally.[14]

Similarly, I've been going to the same mechanic for twenty-five years, ever since I bought my first car while a student at Western. Ian, the owner, earned my loyalty by being straight-up

---

14 And, in one of my bigger life crises, she's nearing retirement and I'm probably never going to get my hair cut again. Fortunately, big hair seems to be making a comeback, although I might need a comb-over by then anyway, based on my family genetics.

honest. He did a fine job getting my rather rusty Chevy on the road, and he has continued to do the same with all the vehicles I have driven since.

There isn't a chance in you-know-where that I'm going to have Octavia service my car, and under no circumstances would I ever want Ian to cut my hair. Nor would I want either of them to do brain surgery should the need arise. Similarly, I'm not going to have one of Canada's finest neurosurgeons fix my car or do my hair — she might be able to shave my head (I suppose it is a skill related to brain surgery), but on the off chance I want a perm, she's probably not the right person for the job.

As funny as this all seems, there is a serious message I want to send: These folks are amazing at what they do. They all got there through training, hard work, and many hours perfecting their craft. The same is true in my industry, and it's important that you understand how to find the right professional to work with you.

What Is the Role of a Certified Financial Planner or CFP®?

The financial planning world is an alphabet soup of professional designations and it can be hard to know what they all mean, let alone what they stand for. One of the designations I hold is Certified Financial Planner, or CFP®. As CFP professionals®, our role is much like that of your family doctor in relation to your overall health care — we are the nexus of your financial care. Our job is to know you and be your advocate as you work through the financial system.

Not every investment or insurance provider has a CFP certification. To become a CFP professional, you need to have several years of industry experience, go through rigorous training, and demonstrate your planning skills. To me, this is what makes the difference between a salesperson and a planner.

CFP professionals have different areas of expertise. For example, I specialize in working with people who have been chronic savers and now find themselves with significant tax issues that will have an impact on their estate. In particular, we're exceptionally good at using charitable giving to minimize taxation.

A good financial planner will start with a deep dive into your personal value system, before making recommendations on investments or insurance. Over the years, I have taken on many clients with strong environmental or social values who were shocked to learn that their pre-existing investment portfolio had been actively invested in companies whose activities violated those values. A good planner will know your values and apply them to every aspect of your portfolio and planning work.

In the last few years, some of the regulatory bodies in Canada have discussed clamping down on who can call themselves a financial planner. Believe it or not, at the time of writing this book, there are virtually no regulations about the qualifications your investment advisor needs to have in order to use this title. Personally, I am looking forward to the day where my profession requires recognized and comprehensive credentials, so that consumers can see a clear distinction between an investment salesperson and a true financial planner.

Getting a Good Estate Lawyer

Another key piece is to ensure that when you do your will, you go to a specialist estate lawyer. While any lawyer can help you draft a proper will, you want to spend your time and money working with someone who specializes in estates. A specialist who is experienced and up-to-date on all of the latest rules may charge you marginally more to draft your will but could potentially save you thousands by having better wording[15] and by anticipating problems that a general-practice lawyer may not have picked up on. Think of it this way: Wouldn't you want someone who is going to be too thorough to draft your last testament to the world, rather than someone who isn't going to put much thought into it? I sure would.

When my wife, Bridget, and I last had our wills redone, our estate lawyer asked us about a number of situations that neither of us had previously contemplated. All of them were great questions. As the saying goes, you don't know what you don't know. With all the work I do in this area, you might think that I could have anticipated every possibility. Nope—not even close. Our lawyer came up with several scenarios I never would have thought of; she had lots of great questions that we had not considered on our own, but we immediately realized they were crucial items the second she voiced them.

---

15 In my home province of Ontario, unclear wording in a will can lead to a contested estate — and the estate itself is potentially on the hook for all legal bills related to poor wording. Costs can reach six figures in some extreme cases!

Ask Around for Your Local Experts

No matter where you live, there will be well-qualified profession-als. The hard part, however, is finding them. Start by looking for your local estate planning council and asking who its members are. Most cities have these councils, which are designed to bring together specialists from a variety of different disciplines related to estate planning: legal, accounting, investment, insurance, and char-itable giving. If you have strong philanthropic interests, your local chapter of the Canadian Association of Gift Planners (CAGP) is another great resource at www.cagp-acpdp.org.

There is no doubt that estate-planning advice will cost you money, and the larger and more complex your estate, the higher that expense will be. Still, the cost of good advice is a small frac-tion of your total asset base. That wise, modest investment can save you, your estate, and your beneficiaries a huge amount of money in the long run.

Just don't ask your estate planner to do your brain surgery or fix your car!

10

What Happens If Your Kid Gets Struck by a Meteorite?

Most of the time, everything is pretty straightforward and routine in the financial planning field, but sometimes we have weird weeks in our office. Prime among them was a call from our client Dede, who told us that her son had just been struck by a meteorite the size of a golf ball! Now, you might be wondering, how did she know it was a meteorite? Well, it was still hot and smoking, and it fell from the sky. Based on the pictures she sent me, at first glance I was pretty sure, too, that it was a meteorite.[16]

---

16 Keep reading to see what it was. Truth is stranger than fiction. Plus, a bit of dramatic tension will likely keep you reading this chapter just to find out what happened.

The reason Dede called us was not that William was injured (fortunately, he was all right—although, needless to stay, a bit surprised!). Instead, she called knowing that I'm a member of the Royal Astronomical Society and could probably point her toward people who would help preserve the meteorite and perhaps be interested in some scientific research. I was happy to do so.

Dede's call was a good — if somewhat unusual — reminder that strange, unexpected things can happen that we probably can't foresee.[17]

Plan for the Unexpected

While it's true you can't predict every possible outcome when doing the work of financial and estate planning, there are three main steps you can take to ensure that you plan for unexpected events and emergencies:

1. Everyone should have an emergency fund. You never know when you might need to tap into cash quickly. If you can't get at it in twenty-four hours or less — it's not an emergency fund! Although being hit by a meteorite won't likely happen to you, I can almost guarantee that something else you can't predict will.

2. Your planning work should look at what happens if you or another family member gets sick. Disability and/or critical illness insurance can, and often should, be important parts of your plan during your working years.

---

17 Interestingly, the odds of you being hit by a meteorite have been calculated, or at least estimated: depending on the assumptions, we all have a lifetime chance of somewhere between 1 in 3,200 to 1 in 840,000,000 ... might be time for little William to buy a lottery ticket!

3. Your planning work should take into account what happens if you, or someone close to you, were to pass away. This is where life insurance is so important — in your working years to replace lost income, and in your later years to offset tax on your estate. Imagine for a moment if William had been unlucky enough to be killed by the meteorite, and the effect it would have had on his family. I don't know any parent who has lost a child who was able to return to work as if nothing had happened.

Protecting Your Kids and Grandkids

In today's society, it can be argued that many of us have gone overboard in protecting our kids. That may be true of being over-protective parents in everyday life, but I find that way too few financial plans address adequately protecting our children in case of dire circumstances.

One of the funniest memories of the birth of my youngest son is that I managed to get a life insurance application in for him less than twenty-four hours after he was born.[18] Our son was born Sunday afternoon, and I handed the application in at the office by eight o'clock the next morning. One of my colleagues looked at me incredulously and simply said, "Paranoid much?" as I handed in the paperwork. My reply: "Yep!"

As much as my colleague made fun of me, after almost twenty years of doing financial planning work, I've seen my fair share of

---

18   Yep, that's right, I'm that kind of guy!

kids with a variety of health issues that have a lifelong impact. I knew my little guy came out healthy and had a clean application — so I loaded him up with insurance, along with a rider enabling him to purchase more coverage in the future without having to provide his medical history. I figure it's the best gift I could have given him for the day of his birth.

I'm a firm believer that every child should have a life insurance policy, as I've seen many children over the years develop health issues that may impair their ability to get this protective coverage later in life. Life insurance may seem like overkill and an unnecessary expense for a newborn, but starting a policy early guarantees coverage later in life, no matter the circumstances, and can mean lower premiums in adulthood as well.

I became a believer in this strategy thanks to one of my very early clients, a thirty-year-old mother of two named Nancy. Nancy and I actually were born on the very same day, so I always remembered her birthday. She and I met like clockwork every two years just before our shared birthday, to sign her up for another $3,000 of life insurance.

Yes, you read that correctly. Nancy buys herself life insurance as a gift every two years on her birthday. It may not be what you would do. But for Nancy, it's the best gift for herself, and her kids.

At the age of nineteen, both of Nancy's kidneys abruptly failed, for reasons that doctors weren't able to fully diagnose at the time. She was rushed onto a transplant list, and eventually a non-related donor was found. Unfortunately, the recipients of unrelated kidney-donor transplants are not normally able to get any kind of life insurance coverage. The few companies that do provide coverage to folks with this medical history are, as you might imagine, prohibitively expensive.

Luckily, Nancy's parents had bought a life insurance policy for her at birth. That policy was for $3,000, which seemed like a huge amount in 1974. (In today's dollars, that's about $15,000, or roughly the cost of a funeral.) Fortunately for Nancy, that policy also had a rider that guaranteed she could increase the amount of coverage by $3,000 every two years without having to provide any medical details.

Fast-forward thirty years, and here is Nancy with two kids of her own, a mortgage, and car payments. In her words, if anything happened to her, her husband was "screwed." The only insurance Nancy had was the policy that her dad had set up for her, plus twice her salary at work, and the extra $3,000 she could add every two years. It was not, she said, enough to cover much of anything if she were to pass away.

That moment, and the concern in Nancy's voice, has always stuck with me. That's why each of my kids has $250,000 of insurance coverage on them, with an option to pick up another $1.2 million in total over their lifetime. That should be enough money to make a sizable impact for my grandkids, should anything happen to one of my boys.

Beyond thinking about your child's future needs, however, there is another more pressing reason to insure your child. While no parent wants to contemplate losing their child, it does happen;

of course, no amount of money can ever compensate for such a terrible loss, but at least life insurance would provide the financial resources to allow your family some time to grieve. For many of us, this situation is too horrible to contemplate; however, I have seen it happen many times in my career as a financial planner, and so my advice is to give it some consideration. Buying a substantial amount of life insurance for a healthy newborn might be paranoid, but it is also highly practical.[19] Kids are usually easy and inexpensive to insure, so buying them coverage early costs little and has a major benefit to their lives later on. Any life insurance policy placed on a child should ideally have a "guaranteed insurability rider" that allows them to purchase more insurance as an adult without having to give medical evidence.[20]

From a tax-planning point of view, insurance policies owned by you that cover your child or grandchild can be passed tax-free to your child or grandchild later in life — allowing you to transfer wealth efficiently from one generation to the next.

---

19 We take our health for granted, but life sometimes has other plans. In fact, on the very day my youngest was born, I was unable to get any more insurance myself because a year before I had had a medical emergency. The doctors were 90 percent convinced that it was a side effect of medication I was on at the time, but there was a 10 percent chance it could have been caused by an undetected tumour. No insurance company was prepared to take me on until I had been free and clear of symptoms for two years, so even I had to wait to increase my coverage until my son was a year old.

20 I'm exceptionally grateful to have had this in place for all of our children, especially given that one of our kids has a medical condition that will likely make it hard for him to get insurance as an adult.

Meteorite-proof Financial Safety Helmets

At the end of the day, a rock hurtling to earth at a speed of seventy-one kilometres per hour from space is such an unlikely event, William may be the only person you ever hear of in your lifetime who gets hits by one.[21] That said, if you stop for a moment and create a list of unexpected and unusual things that have happened to people you know and love, I imagine that list would be quite lengthy. I think it is safe to say we will all have one or two things in our lives that will hit us or our family out of the blue and have a major impact in our lives. As astronomers, and financial planners, we wish for clear skies — but we plan for clouds, just in case.

---

21 In a twist worthy of an M. Night Shamalan movie, it turned out it wasn't a meteorite but a piece of lava rock that had fallen from the sky — although the nearest volcano is on the other side of North America. It was a very weird week indeed!

11

The Greatest Gift You Can Give Is Being Prepared

L et's face it, it's human nature to avoid what makes us uncomfortable. Sometimes, though, dealing with the uncomfortable is exactly what we need to do. Our office recently received a strong reminder of this painful lesson.

Not too long ago, one of our client families suffered the sudden loss of someone we'll call Joe. It was a tough day for us in the office, as we're very fond of Joe's family, who are all wonderful people. It also wasn't a stretch to put ourselves in their shoes, as Joe was a relatively young person in the prime of his life; a loving son, husband, and father; and a professional who was a provider for his family. He was about the same age as many of us in our firm, and as we received the news, one of our employees was weeks away from having twins. Family is one of our strongest values — and we were witnessing one of our client families being torn apart by a tragic loss.

Fortunately, Joe had recently taken the time to update the beneficiary designations in his will and life insurance policy to reflect changes in his family situation. I'm sure that when he did so, he could not have anticipated how timely that small but important action was. His family certainly is grateful for what he had done only a few weeks before his untimely death.

When Did You Last Review Your Will and Powers of Attorney?

If it's been more than four years, pull out these documents and take a read through them. You might be surprised at how much in your life has changed since you last updated them. You might find you need to make some minor, or even major, updates. Confirm that your executor is still willing and able to serve. Check the guardianship of your kids and make sure any charities you have listed have their official legal name shown properly. Since 2014, major changes have been made to federal and provincial laws that apply to estate planning; if your will predates that, it is worth having a conversation with your lawyer as soon as possible to find out if your situation is affected.

Who Are Your Named Beneficiaries?

Not long ago, I reviewed an insurance policy for another one of our clients — and quickly realized the beneficiary had passed away two years before! Clearly an update was needed. One of the best things Joe did was to update the beneficiary designations on his policies just before he passed away.[22] This simple action took almost no time and ensured that his family was protected and provided for financially.

And life insurance policies are not the only things you should check and update. RRSPs, RRIFs, TFSAs, and company pension plans all allow you to name a beneficiary to whom the assets will flow in the event of your death. Review all of these at least annually to ensure that you are leaving your legacy to the right people.

Do You Have the Right Amount of Life Insurance?

Your need for insurance coverage changes throughout your lifetime, and rarely is this number static. If you have young children and a mortgage, most likely you need a "whack-load" (to use my very technical term) of term insurance, as did Joe. However, the insurance need you have in your thirties and forties is very different in nature than the amount and type of coverage you might need for estate planning later in life to deal with taxation on your estate, for example.

If you're between fifty and sixty-five, you probably need to take a close look at your insurance and make sure it's doing what you need it to, as you are likely transitioning to retirement. Too often, people forget to make the necessary changes at a young

---

22 Generally — and Joe was no exception — you can't time this very well, unless you have a terminal illness. Make this review a yearly habit.

enough age and find their options become severely limited and costly. If you make changes in the fifteen years before your retirement, you'll most likely find the cost much lower, and you will enter your retirement years much better prepared.

Where Are All Your Important Documents Kept?

All the estate planning in the world will be useless if you don't let your family, your executor, and your Power of Attorney (POA) know where you keep your will and POA documents. That may sound obvious, but it is surprising the number of families I have met over the years who can't find them when needed. The implications can be disastrous if you don't let your survivors know where these key legal documents are.

I worked with a family many years ago where the mother never told the rest of the family where her will was kept. After two years of searching, the province declared that there was no will, and the estate was distributed according to a provincial formula, which worked out to be less than ideal. The beneficiaries had to wait years to receive funds, and the breakdown of who received what was not at all what the family had in mind.

Marriage Invalidates a Will; Separation/Divorce Do Not

In Ontario and some other provinces, your will is declared null and void as soon as you are married (or remarried). This makes sense, because you have legal obligations to your new spouse; however, most folks don't realize that neither separation nor divorce invalidates a will. Do you want the bulk of your estate going to someone from whom you have split? I didn't think so. It is vital to update your will as soon as you separate from your spouse or partner; and it's equally important to create a new will when you enter into a new spousal relationship.

Have You Told Your Advisors about Important Changes in Your Life?

Major changes in your life (new job, marriage, births, inheritance, etc.) all can have a major impact on the advice we professionals give. One of the best things Joe did in the year before he died was to update me on some major changes in his life. We could then reflect those changes in his financial and estate plans to make sure his family was appropriately protected. And it's not only your financial planner who needs to know what's going on in your life; be sure to communicate the same information to all the advisors you work with: lawyers, accountants, trust officers, and others.

As your financial planner, if I don't know about changes in your life, I can't help. Keeping an open line of communication to us, your professional advisors, allows us to deliver much better value. We can help you anticipate things you might not even be considering at key times of your life.

What Are You Waiting For?

Joe's loss was tragic, and he will be greatly missed. Luckily, the changes Joe happened to make to his financial and estate plans just weeks before his death did protect his family after his sudden passing and made a terrible time in their lives a lot less stressful than it otherwise would have been. For that, we were all grateful.

As humans, we have a tendency to avoid doing the things that make us uncomfortable, even if we know we should. But there is a real danger in leaving the difficult issues and discussions around estate planning too long. If Joe had done that, things would have turned out very differently for his family. Don't put your own family at risk; face those uncomfortable conversations and decisions head-on. Think of the peace of mind you'll have, knowing that your family is provided for, no matter what lies ahead.

Provided you take the time now, someday your family will thank you when you are gone, just as Joe's family thanked him.

12

How to Avoid a Family War

I t's been said many times that memories are more important than money. In the first few months of my career as a financial planner, I had an eye-opening meeting with a client, a lady in her forties named Rachel, who has forever burned that saying into my mind. I first met Rachel when I took over her accounts after a colleague retired. In her client file, I found a rather intriguing note that simply said, "Make sure you ask her about the art collection."[23]

Families have all kinds of traditions. It could be a favourite recipe, a song, or a trip to the cottage — but in Rachel's case, she came from a long line of artists and art collectors. Four generations

---

23 Never underestimate the importance of leaving people cryptic notes. Some of the greatest and most interesting conversations I have had with clients have started with mysterious notes in the file.

of her family had made a tradition of collecting paintings. The history of each painting was passed down from generation to generation, along with the actual artwork itself. Each member of the family would proudly hang the part of the collection they'd inherited, ensuring that the art always remained on display to be enjoyed.

By the time the collection made it to Rachel's mother, nearly fifty pieces of art adorned her house. Some were valuable in monetary terms, but the real value of the collection was in the stories around how each piece was acquired and the history of the past owners within the family. The tradition was nearly a century old by the time Rachel was born. It was an incredible family legacy that Rachel and her three siblings looked forward to continuing.

Rachel's mom passed away, and her dad went on to remarry a few years later. In the process, he rewrote his will (because marriage invalidates any previous will here in Ontario) to ensure that while most of his assets would go to his new wife, the art collection would be split equally among his kids. And that, you would think, would have been the end of it.[24]

Rachel's dad developed dementia a few years later, along with congestive heart failure. In the last few months of his life, the relationship between his new wife and his children deteriorated as the stress of caregiving took a heavy toll on all parties.

In the last few days of his life, Rachel's dad handwrote a new

---

24 You could think that, but it never, ever is. That's why people in my line of work will never be replaced by robots.

will (called a holograph will), which stated that all of his assets were to go to his new wife, and none to his children. Rachel and her siblings were understandably upset. While they wanted no monetary inheritance, they were mortified that the family art collection would also now be inherited by their stepmom. To add insult to injury, their stepmother had often made derogatory comments about many of the pieces and loathed the entire collection. Rachel believed that her stepmom may have found it a constant reminder of her husband's first marriage.

Holograph wills are legal in Ontario; however, they are often subject to a number of legal uncertainties. In this case, Rachel and her siblings were concerned that their dad was not legally capable of making a will as he was dying, particularly in light of his cognitive decline and concerns they had about undue influence being exercised upon him in the last few days of his life by their stepmom. The entire mess ended up in court and, on the day I met Rachel, it had been ongoing for nearly two-and-a-half years![25]

By the time everything had finally settled, a judge did indeed find that Rachel's dad was not legally capable of changing his will when he did and that the stepmom had most likely been in a position of undue influence in encouraging him to do so. By that point, however, massive legal costs — as well as substantial bills from caring for Dad in the last few months of his life — had

---

25 One of the more interesting quirks of the estate laws in Ontario is that if someone contests a will for a valid reason, then the deceased's estate is on the hook for all legal costs. As you can imagine, the legal bills on a multi-year court battle can add up quickly.

drained all the cash from the estate, requiring a number of the paintings to be sold at auction before the estate could be dispersed. Five long years after their dad passed away, Rachel and her siblings shared the ten or so paintings left in the collection. It was a sad, bitter end to a battle that could — and should — have been avoided. With proper planning in advance, the family art collection could no doubt have been saved.

In unique circumstances like this, it is often worth paying more to have a specialist draw up your will, as it could possibly save thousands of dollars of legal costs down the road, like those incurred in Rachel's story. Specialist estate lawyers see many complex and unusual situations arise over their years of practice, and they can plan accordingly for them. I suspect if an estate lawyer had drawn up Rachel's parents' wills, he or she would have made inquiries about this kind of family legacy and suggested several possible ways to ensure a smooth transfer:

1. Rachel's mother could have gifted the art collection directly to the children in her will, rather than leaving all assets to her husband. This way, the art never would have eventually formed part of his estate.

2. Alternatively, a trust could have been set up, in which the art could have been left for the enjoyment of Rachel's dad, but ownership would then revert to the children at his death.

3. Finally, Rachel's mother could have simply begun gifting the art during her lifetime.

You may not have an art collection like Rachel's family did, but there are likely items you own that have more than monetary meaning to you and your family. It's worth having a conversation with your lawyer about these items next time you update your own will — after all, you don't want your legacy to be one of family warfare.

13

Harry
the Waiter

L ike all parents, I love my kids, even in those moments
when I might want to strangle them. If you are a parent,
I'm sure you have had this moment as well.[26] The relationship between parent and child is complex, and has many, many lay-
ers. This was hammered home to me while I was driving recently,
listening to the CBC Radio podcast *Love Me*, which featured an
episode called "The Way We Were." The episode features a woman
who was forced to report her own teenaged son to the police after
he stole significant amounts of money from her bank account. She

---

26 My friend Sara once posted on her Facebook feed: "Today I understood for the
first time why so many animals choose to eat their own young." Our mutual friends
without children were horrified, while those of us with kids simply nodded our heads
wisely, quietly thinking about the times we felt the same but didn't have her courage
to say it so publicly!

does an incredible job talking about the complex emotions of loving your child despite the complete loss of trust.

When Your Kids Love Your Money More than They Love You

A few years ago, an article in *Maclean's* magazine talked about the complex interplay between generations when it comes to inheritance. As a planner, I've pretty much seen it all over my career. I've seen both the selfless and the greedy when it comes to families, and no two situations are alike.

The article in *Maclean's* contained one of my favourite quotes of all time about estate planning. A lawyer is recounting a meeting with a very well-dressed couple in his office. When he asked what they did for a living, the wife replied, "Oh, Harry's not going to tell you this, but he's a waiter." The lawyer asked at what restaurant, and she replied, "Not that kind of waiter. He's waiting for his inheritance!" It turned out that, in this case, Harry was already spending his inheritance — but in advance. It is a situation that we see more and more often in our practice.

In 2006, Decima Research completed an interesting study, which looked at how much inheritance the average Canadian expected, versus what they actually received — and it's quite the gap. On average, people expected an inheritance of just over $150,000. The reality, though, was that in Canada at that time, the average inheritance was only $56,000. This means that your kids might be expecting an inheritance three times larger than they will actually receive. If their own planning is dependent upon unrealistic expectations of what they will inherit, they will be in for a big shock when the time comes. The moral of the story is that it is very dangerous to live your lifestyle assuming a future inheritance will "rescue" you from your current overspending. I wish more people truly understood this hard, cold fact.

You Don't Actually Have to Give Your Kids Anything

One little-known fact of estate planning (at least here in Ontario) is that you are not legally obligated to provide anything for your children in your will. The exception, however, is that if someone is financially dependent on you, you are obligated to provide support if you pass away, and a court can override your will and other beneficiary arrangements, such as life insurance or RRSPs/RRIFs, if you have not arranged to provide the necessary support.

So, be careful. If you are financially supporting your adult children on a regular basis and haven't put them in your estate plans, it's entirely possible that they could take your estate to court to receive a piece of the pie. The test is based on their financial relationship with you, not on your role as a parent. And, most importantly, if you don't provide for them sufficiently in your will, they can tie up the funds for years. They may even deplete the value of your estate thanks to the legal costs your estate may have to incur to fight this sort of battle. In this case, the other people or causes you may want to leave money to could receive far less than you intend.

As always, it's essential to have a discussion with your kids ahead of time to be clear about your plans and intentions, and about their expectations. And it's critical to seek legal advice when there are complex family dynamics at play; your lawyer might save your estate a whole lot of money and headaches where your kids are involved.

14

How to
Delicately Cover Your
Assets with a POA

I have a great love of music and a warped sense of humour. It may come as no surprise, then, that I'm a huge Monty Python fan. One of my all-time favourite short films is *Romance with a Double Bass*, from 1974, starring John Cleese and his then-wife Connie Booth. The movie is based on an Anton Chekhov short story about a rather hapless double-bass player from the royal court and the princess, both of whom coincidentally find themselves skinny-dipping in the same lake at the same time. Much wonderful comedy occurs in their attempt to sneak the princess back into the castle inside his double-bass case with her dignity still (mainly) intact.[27]

---

27 If you've never seen this charming movie, you should check it out — but be warned, it includes plot-driven nudity and far more of John Cleese than you've ever seen (or may want to see).

Unfortunately, salvaging your finances doesn't involve as much hilarity as our little film, nor does it involve anything as simple as a double-bass case. Life is far too good at throwing curveballs that can have a disastrous effect on your financial situation. I'm not talking here about the things you have control over (like getting in to, or out of, debt), but rather, other things over which you have little to no control. Imagine for a moment a situation where your accounts are frozen by your bank once they find out you are in a coma. Who will pay your bills, your mortgage, or your insurance? Each of these has consequences if payment is not made. If you are in such circumstances for a while, your financial situation can become quite dire.

Financially speaking, I hope you are never caught with your pants down. If you are, fixing the situation is stressful, and rarely humorous. The good news is that there is a vital tool available to you so you can set up your financial affairs and plan for the worst of circumstances while things are still working great: the power of attorney (POA). Unlike a will, a POA designation is for when "you aren't dead yet" but are otherwise incapable or unable to make decisions on your own behalf. They are an essential planning tool because once you are over the age of eighteen, no other person, unless empowered by a POA, can act on your behalf where your money is involved.

In Ontario, there are two types of POAs: one for property (which includes your financial affairs) and another for health care. Each is a separate document, and it's absolutely vital you have both in place. Rather than talking about the specifics of each of these documents, I want to highlight some lessons around the practical uses of POAs that I've learned as a financial planner over the years.

Make Sure Your POAs Are Accessible

As obvious as this sounds, it's actually the most important thing I can tell you: make sure the people you have appointed as your "attorneys" know where to find copies of your POA documents. I once worked with a family whose mother had locked hers in a safety deposit box, but the bank branch had closed years before and no one had any idea how to track down the box contents. Eventually, the court had to be involved to appoint a family member to look after their mom's affairs.

If you become incapacitated without having a POA in place, someone would have to get the Office of the Public Guardian and Trustee (OPGT) in your home province to intercede. They are the attorney of last resort. While it is possible for your family to request permission from the courts and the OPGT to be appointed guardian over your affairs, the process is time-consuming and often expensive — and by then, much financial damage may already be done to your affairs.

Two Vital Words: The Importance of "or" Not "and" with Joint Attorneys for Health Care

I recently attended a talk by Dr. Natalie Hertzman, Medical Director of St. Joseph's Hospice in London, Ontario. She strongly emphasized to the audience that, in her experience, many medical situations require immediate decisions. As a palliative care doctor, she has seen families unable to get confirmation in a timely fashion when there are POAs who have been appointed jointly, leading to compromises in the medical care of the family member.

If your health care POA document says "John *and* Susan," the doctors must get consent from *both* POAs before any action can be taken. If John isn't available, Susan has no authority and vice versa. On the other hand, if it says, "John *or* Susan," then either John *or* Susan can give instructions independent of one another and the doctors can act immediately.

Family Members Have No Right to Financial Information Just Because They're Family

If we have one constant issue with POA situations in our office, it's that most people assume that if they're immediate family, they're entitled to information. This simply isn't true. If you are over the age of majority, no one can act on your behalf or gain information about your accounts and other financial affairs unless you have made them your POA for property or else a court has granted them authority.

As a financial planner, some of the most uncomfortable conversations I've had are about this topic. Part of the confusion comes from the fact that, for health care, in the absence of a POA, family does have some legal right to make decisions, but the same does not hold true for finances.

Sometimes, Family Is Not the Best Choice

Sometimes it's not the best idea to make a family member a POA. Take a business owner, for instance. In my case, my wife is the POA for my personal financial affairs, but I have a corporate POA appointed for my ownership interest in my company. Why? Bridget is a teacher, not a financial professional and, therefore, it would take her a huge amount of time and effort to get up to speed on all the regulatory and other requirements of the business if she were to have to step in as POA.

I'm comfortable appointing a trust company to handle my business interests, as they have staff who are trained on corporate rules and responsibilities. It's way easier and more efficient to delegate this task to them. I've made provisions that, if my corporate POA is activated, they do need to consult with Bridget and honour her wishes when possible, but the legal responsibility falls to them, not her.

Being Prepared for the Spanish Inquisition

As much as (according to John Cleese) no one expects the Spanish Inquisition, if you are acting as a POA you have certain legal obligations to document your actions, in case there are any challenges at a later date. Additionally, the POA cannot co-mingle the funds of the person on whose behalf they are acting with their own funds. If you have appointed a family member, they need to be aware of their legal obligations.

POA arrangements are complicated at the best of times, and most often are active during the worst of times. It is vitally important that you put thought and care into your own power of attorney arrangements and you work with a well-qualified lawyer to draft it. These documents are incredibly powerful and, in the wrong hands, could lead to disaster. In the right hands, they quite literally may save your life.

At the end of the day, you don't want to be caught with your financial pants down, hiding behind a double bass. Make sure you check that your POA arrangements are up-to-date and effective for your circumstances. If you do, then you'll "always look on the bright side of life!"

Part 3

Building Wealth to Create Your Legacy

Just as important as ensuring you have taken steps to protect your legacy, is doing a good job of growing it in the first place. In this section, we will explore how to maximize your wealth through smart investing, clever tax planning, and knowing where the risks lie in your portfolio — all based, as before, on the entertaining and enlightening stories of clients with whom I have worked. There's a lot to be learned from the experiences of other folks much like you.

15

Grow Your Wealth by Giving It Away

I'm sure your first thought reading the title of this chapter is that I am crazy — and that this sounds like a strange way to start a section about growing your wealth. While it is entirely possible that I am crazy (my wife is nodding sagely in the background as I write this section), it turns out that the title of this chapter has actually been scientifically proven to be true.

Professor Russell James of Texas Tech University published a study in 2009 in *The Journal of Educational Advancement* based on ten years of data on US-based individuals. In this study, James analyzed the data of over twenty-eight thousand people and discovered that those who had active charitable-giving plans grew their net worth at a rate of 50-to-100 percent higher than those who did not. That is a pretty significant difference.

Now, you might be thinking: *Well, older people with more money would have taken the time to plan, so what is the big deal?* The amazing part of his findings was that his study was looking at the growth of net worth relative to when people started doing charitable planning, and it accounted for differences in initial wealth and age. In research, we like to say that correlation doesn't mean causality, but in this case, my own experience leads me to think that Professor James's findings do point to the likelihood that undertaking planning earlier in life to incorporate a charitable-giving strategy will grow your wealth.

I've worked with all kinds of folks over the years, and one thing that has struck me has been how much working in, volunteering with, and contributing financially to the non-profit sector leads to a net benefit for all who are involved. Provided, of course, that one is truly giving selflessly and not for the sake of personal gain.

First and foremost, in my mind, is that people who are inclined to support charity are almost always amazing, warm, compassionate people.[28] Since, by definition, charity is a selfless act, selfish people generally don't show up to the ball game; and certainly, the odd time they do, they don't feel welcome at the table, and quickly leave.

In my own professional financial planning practice, we have actually used philanthropy as a filter to help decide who we do

---

28   Jerks just don't survive long around a charity. The nice folks who volunteer and work for charities can smell a jerk a mile away, and they generally don't tolerate anything less than awesomeness when it comes to personality and behaviour.

business with: if you aren't at all interested in incorporating charitable giving into your financial and estate plans, or aren't giving of your time to volunteer, we are not the firm for you. It was amazing, once I made the decision to focus in this area, how quickly my practice filled with kind, warm, generous clients.

People who value and practice charity are prepared to make short-term personal sacrifices for the long-term collective good. And, based on what I've seen, the universe seems to be very good at providing long-term payoff for those willing to give of themselves in the now.

People who give to charity, be it their time or money, tend to build networks and trust as their long-term commitments develop. If you stop and think for a moment, I am sure you can immediately think of who in your social circle exhibits deep personal integrity and compassion, people you hold in high regard. These, on the whole, are the kind of people we all prefer to associate with, do business with, and whom we know we can count on. We all love to get to know people like this.

It should come as no surprise that these kinds of people will have better financial prospects than those with a different set of personality traits. If you were an employer, wouldn't you be more inclined to offer these people a job? If one of these people owns or runs a business, wouldn't you prefer to put your business with them rather than a competitor with a different set of values? And, to add a little more zest to the sauce, isn't this kind of person more likely to lead a lifestyle that is less consumer-driven and, therefore, likely more inclined to save money at a higher rate?

The traditional perception of philanthropy has been that some rich person has money and gives it away, maybe getting their name on a hospital wing, university fund, or some other public recognition; but both my experience and Dr. James's research point to a very different reality. There are millions of ordinary people living much more modest lifestyles to whom philanthropy is an important priority, and they reflect this in their financial plans and daily actions, quietly and generously giving of what they have to help others. And it turns out that that mindset of abundance creates abundance — in their lives and in the lives they touch. Giving really does make you richer — not just in spirit, but literally also, in wealth.

16

The Baker and the Roller Coaster

Early in my career as a financial planner, I took over the accounts of a wonderful gentleman, a baker named Daryl. As you might expect, given his profession, Daryl could make dough rise like nobody's business — and he could do so in multiple ways, it turns out. Despite never earning more than $50,000 a year (in today's dollars), he had managed to tuck away nearly a million dollars by the time he reached his late fifties.

When I met Daryl, he had, in his own words "just gotten over changing his underwear daily," having ridden through the stock market collapse of 2001. A fairly aggressive investor, he had been hammered by the significant drops in equity markets.

Burned by his experience, he came to me looking for a more moderate portfolio that wouldn't be as volatile as the one he had built, and wouldn't give him as wild a ride as the one he'd recently experienced. He was determined to retire by sixty, but the drop in his portfolio value had made that an unlikely goal. A bit of a gambler by nature, he had turned quite conservative after having been so badly burned. I took Daryl through a risk-tolerance exercise and, sure enough, he needed to adjust his holdings to a significantly more conservative arrangement, which we did.

Two years later, Daryl came back for a visit. Still keenly watching the stock markets, he noted that the year before, the Toronto Stock Exchange Index was up 19.3 percent, and he wanted to switch everything over to invest 100 percent in equities again. The good news in the markets made him forget how he had felt only a short while before, when his portfolio had been routed by two bad years of negative returns.

I pulled out the original risk assessment we'd done two years before and compared it to the one we had just done, when he said he was OK with super-high-risk investments. It was the tale of two Daryls — one burned in a downturn and one euphoric in an upturn. "Which one is the truth?" I asked.

Daryl started laughing and said, "OK, you got me!" He sheepishly recalled the terrifying feeling of the panic attacks he'd had two years before, when he thought he was actually having a heart attack, and he decided this time that he should probably be somewhere in the middle, between the two extremes.

The Truth Lies Somewhere in Between

That meeting with Daryl was a great moment for me in understanding our psychology as investors. When markets are up — and have been going up for a long time — we can easily forget what it's like to experience a downturn. There are two ways to evaluate risk: the risk you can afford to take financially, and the type of risk that will keep you up at night, thinking about firing your investment representative.

While I would love to tell you to focus on the first one, I often find that it's the second one — the emotional side, thinking with your heart — that truly determines the amount of risk you should actually take. As a financial planner, I'm always OK with you taking less risk and sleeping better at night. No one should have to stare at the ceiling worrying all night long while the second hand on the clock ticks slower and slower beside you as you think about investment markets.

In fact, beware of falling into the trap of pursuing high returns no matter what. Make sure you realize at a fundamental level that super-high returns probably also mean you could have super-high losses. It's OK to give up on one in order to avoid the other. At the end of the day, money is just a tool to be used — not something that should negatively affect the quality of your life.

Like Daryl, the risk you should take might lie somewhere between the extremes you feel in down or up markets. There are lots of ways you can work with your investment representative to make sure your tolerance for risk is sitting in the right place in your portfolio.

If you have opened your investment statements recently and it hasn't been a good year or a good quarter, those results might be keeping you up at night. One simple test is to ask your investment representative what a portfolio similar to yours did during the 2008 financial crisis. If you're OK with the answer, your portfolio is probably structured in a way that suits you. Otherwise, if the answer sounds horrifying and makes your heart race — you should probably make some changes sooner rather than later.

Once you get things lined up in a way that lets you sleep at night, I hope you wake up to croissants and pastries for breakfast. I know a guy who can probably supply you with some, if I can convince him to give up the retired life!

17

I Can
See the Future
from Here!

Every night for the last fifteen years, I've read a story to at least one of our kids. The days of them being too old for this will soon be upon us, but for now it's still a wonderful tradition we enjoy very much. We've read thousands of stories over the years, but inevitably the family favourite is anything from *Calvin and Hobbes*, the legendary and timeless comic strip by Bill Watterson.

My favourite strip was published December 30, 1989. In it, Calvin marks the dawn of the new decade with incredulity. In Calvin's words: "Big deal! Where are the flying cars? Where are the moon colonies? Where are the personal robots and the zero-gravity boots, huh?" I can understand where he's coming from.

What's more, it's been almost thirty years since that strip was published and these things still haven't come to pass.[29]

We Can't Predict the Future

As a financial planner, I'm often asked to predict the future. Most of the time, when I tell people what I do for a living, the first question is, "Do you have any hot stock tips?" My answer: "Sure, the markets will do one of three things: go up, go down, or stay the same." Strangely, people usually ask me a second time, thinking I'm hiding something from them, but it is my most honest and professionally accurate answer.

Anyone who tells you they know what the future is going to be for the markets either has an overdeveloped ego or is selling snake oil. As our example from *Calvin and Hobbes* shows, people have been predicting the future for a long time, and they're rarely accurate.

The One Exception

One of the smartest investment managers I've ever met once commented that the only investment standard you can rely on to predict the future is that everything reverts to the average. The real challenge, she said, is knowing what the average is and being patient enough to wait for the valuation to return there. What she meant by this was that sometimes prices for equities (or anything for sale, really) go way above or below what they should be, but

---

29 I, for one, am still incredibly bitter. I'm totally on Calvin's side here.

that, inevitably, they will return to where they should be, based on their long-term rates, relative to the cost to produce. It was probably the most astute piece of advice on investing I've ever been given.

Now, not everyone spends a lot of time looking at investment markets, so let's use an example we're all familiar with — housing prices. Over the last hundred years, housing has increased at about the rate of inflation over the long term. In particular, a reasonable standard over that time period is that a house should be affordable if its cost is three-to-four times the household's annual income. According to a very interesting article in the *Globe and Mail* in April 2017, the average price of a house in the Greater Toronto Area (GTA) in September 2016 was $627,395 — more than eight times the average household income. Worryingly, just after the article was written, the average house price became $919,449, or *twelve* times the average household income in the GTA. At the time of publishing of this book, housing prices in the GTA have retreated a bit — but continue to be well above the average compared to household income.

It doesn't take a lot to imagine that at twelve times the average family's income, house prices are reaching a point where they will have to come down. And, sure enough, housing prices started going down in April 2018, and the most recent data from the Toronto Real Estate Board's website shows prices were dropping over the fall.

So, knowing that the value of investments always reverts to

the average, we know that either incomes have to increase significantly (by about 300 to 400 percent) or housing prices need to drop. I don't think it takes a lot to imagine which is the most likely scenario.

The problem is, I can't tell you when that potential reversion to the average will happen — it could be tomorrow, or it could be in five years. But someday in the future (or by the time you read this book), things will revert to normal, and it's likely to be painful for many GTA homeowners, unless they get some pretty hefty raises at work!

Applying This Principle to Your Non-Real-Estate Investments

One of the most important fundamental aspects of investing is ensuring you rebalance your investments to keep your overall asset allocation on target — the percentage of your total portfolio that you have invested in various investment classes. I build this principle into almost every portfolio I set up for a client.

It's not about what the hot pick is in your portfolio; it's about ensuring your portfolio has the right balance of investments — stocks, bonds, cash, real estate, and other classes — based on your personal financial situation. In short, it's boring investing, not the sexy prediction of the future you likely wanted. But, trust me, it's the hottest investment tip I can give you.

In the meantime, please let me know if you hear of a company doing R&D on those zero-gravity boots Calvin was talking about.

18

Jim's Pension and *Jurassic Park*

I f you're a movie buff, you likely know that one of the hottest movie tickets in the summer of 2018 was yet another *Jurassic Park* movie, in which extinct dinosaurs are brought to life by crazy scientists.[30] In the financial world, there's a creature that's on the verge of extinction as well: the defined-benefit pension plan. As the news cycle has been reminding us recently, there aren't too many of these particular pensions left walking the earth.

With a defined-benefit pension plan, you receive a predetermined percentage of your annual salary for life. These plans are golden because they provide guaranteed income that you can count on until the day you die but, much like the dinosaurs, they

---

30 You would think after five movies where most of the main characters get eaten, they would realize you probably shouldn't have brought dinosaurs back to life, but who am I to judge?

are nearly extinct in many private-sector workplaces because of the high cost to employers. This trend serves as a strong reminder that many things we take for granted in our financial life do not have an unlimited lifespan — and that includes guaranteed money for life in retirement.

Today, the dinosaur of the defined-benefit pension has evolved into the more common defined-contribution plan, which looks and acts a lot like your RRSP. It is still called a pension— and subject to the same restrictive pension rules and laws as a defined-benefit plan — but the amount of the income to be provided in retirement is not known in advance, nor is it guaranteed. Defined-contribution plans are far more popular with employers than defined-benefit pension plans because they cost a lot less, but they are potentially not as good for employees because they lack the guarantee of a stable income for life.

Still, for people lucky enough to be part of any plan, a pension is at the heart of their retirement income. One of our clients, Jim, has worked hard his whole life to earn that benefit. Every paycheque, money goes into his pension plan, paid for by Jim and his employer. When he retires, he believes that he can look forward to having 70 percent of his income replaced by his work pension.[31]

Life is going to be good! Or is it? Jim came to me recently to try and figure this out, because his employer had offered him an early retirement package and he wanted to determine if it would be financially viable to take it and retire early.

---

31   Or so he thinks!

The Fossilizing Nest Egg

Unfortunately, once we started looking at the details, Jim's pension started to look like a real velociraptor's breakfast. Unlike many companies in days of yore, Jim's employer doesn't have a defined-benefit plan, which as you recall provides a fixed amount in retirement. In Jim's case, his employer moved to a defined-contribution plan, which sounds like a pension but in reality works a lot like an RRSP: Jim saves money in the plan and his employer matches his contributions, then he chooses his investments from a selection of offerings, and he gets whatever the balance happens to be at retirement.

Jim's retirement is depending on those funds, but he has to hope there isn't going to be a major market downturn that will decrease the value of those investments. If the portfolio built from his defined-contribution plan doesn't perform as well as he's counting on, he might have to hold off his retirement a bit longer. We've encouraged him to move a chunk of his holdings to cash as retirement draws nearer, while we sort out the long-term plan. We know his funds are sufficient right now to handle a long retirement — but they might not be if a market downturn happens. If Jim had a defined-benefit pension plan, this wouldn't even be a concern to him.

Who Doesn't Want a Gold-plated Pension Plan?

Let's be honest — most of us would love a defined-benefit pension plan, but most employers no longer offer them because of the high potential cost. These gold-plated pensions are becoming extremely expensive to fund, as retired employees are living longer and interest rates have dropped to record lows in the last decade. In fact, unless you are a public-sector employee, these plans are as rare as a stegosaurus is these days. Fortunately for Jim, there is another option: use some of the pension to buy an annuity.

An annuity is basically a "purchased" defined-benefit pension plan. You go to an insurer (or, sometimes for non-registered money, a charity that you also want to donate to) and give them a lump sum in return for guaranteed income for the rest of your life. Think of it as the inverse of life insurance.

A lot of people I talk to don't like annuities at first glance, as there is the potential with an annuity to have nothing left for the estate. Ironically, though, most of these folks, when asked, say they wish they had a defined-benefit pension plan. In fact, buying an annuity is essentially purchasing your own gold-plated defined-benefit pension plan. For some reason, we have a hard time psychologically making the connection between the two, even though in many ways they are very similar in what they provide.

Is Another Mass-extinction on Its Way?

On June 29, 2018, one of Canada's largest insurers, Manulife, announced that it was no longer going to sell fixed annuities. This may be one of the biggest shockwaves in the investment community in years. While many small insurers have removed certain product lines, up until Manulife's announcement, no major insurance company had removed annuities from their product offering.

For consumers like Jim, this can only be seen as bad news going forward. Less competition usually leads to less-favourable rates; and, potentially, if Manulife doesn't see annuities as a viable business line, other major insurers could be looking at exiting the market as well.

Imagine a world where you can't find a way to get guaranteed income for life. It's scaring Jim, and it's scaring me a bit, too, as a planner. In my experience, the greatest risk in retirement is not how *much* you earn, but how *long* your cash flow will last. We routinely use annuities and defined-benefit pensions to address that longevity risk in retirement plans. Other than those tools (both endangered species at this point), the options are few and far between and usually much more expensive. It's hard to leave a legacy when you have outlived all your own resources!

If, like Jim, you are retired or retiring shortly and don't already have a fixed source of lifelong income in your plans, I encourage you to review your financial plan to see if annuities are a useful tool — before both annuities and defined-benefit pensions go the way of the dinosaur.

19

A Hard Lesson

As Canadians, we are gifted with some pretty good safety nets in our retirement. Aside from universal health care, we have the financial benefits of the Canada Pension Plan, (CPP), Old Age Security (OAS), the Guaranteed Income Supplement (GIS), and a whole variety of government programs. The other part of our retirement safety net comes from private pension plans and disability plans offered by most larger employers. But what happens if your employer goes under? The answer for one person was, unfortunately, disaster.

I met Chris in 2008. He had worked for a company whose name you might recognize: Nortel. It had been an awful decade for Nortel, and most of the company's employees had long since been laid off after the technology bubble of 2001 burst. Chris was one of the lucky ones, though, and had kept his job. But that good fortune wouldn't last; a few years before he became eligible for retirement, some chronic health issues arose, and he found himself unable to work and on long-term disability (LTD).

When I met him, Chris had just turned fifty-five and Nortel had offered him three choices for taking early retirement: retire with a reduced pension; commute his pension and move it away from Nortel (in other words, take the lump-sum value and invest it himself); or stay on LTD until age sixty-five.

Chris hoped that commuting his pension and setting up an annuity would give him more money, as his cash flow was very tight on LTD. He had gotten annuity quotes and, while he would have been marginally better off with an annuity than starting the reduced pension, Chris noted that his pension also came with lifetime medical and dental benefits. In any situation, though, it seemed that he would be far better off to stay on LTD and collect his pension at age sixty-five. It was the right thing for him to do, based on the information that he had available at the time

A year or so later, Nortel declared bankruptcy. In one of the rudest surprises in Canadian employment history, it suddenly became abundantly clear that the safety net at Nortel was virtually non-existent. Unlike most employers with traditional long-term disability plans, Nortel was not using an insurance company to underwrite claims; instead, employees on LTD were being paid directly out of Nortel's ongoing revenues, and the company was simply paying an insurer to administer and adjudicate claims. When Nortel declared bankruptcy, its LTD plan vanished. It turns out that some of the creditors the company was attempting to escape were actually Nortel's own disabled employees.

To add insult to injury, the pension plan was woefully underfunded—Nortel had only funded the plan enough to meet roughly half of its obligations. Bankruptcy allowed Nortel to leave this obligation behind as well, effectively impoverishing every Nortel retiree in the country. And, of course, the third and final insult: the lifetime medical and dental benefits offered to retirees disappeared into thin air as well.

If Only Chris Had Known

Chris had acted on the best information he had available, not knowing the Nortel "house of cards" was going to collapse with such disastrous and far-reaching consequences. Had he commuted his pension, forgone his medical and dental benefits, and retired early, he would have been vastly further ahead than he is today. Ten years later, the court battles around Nortel's pension money continue to make headlines, with some estimates claiming that nearly $2 billion in legal costs have drained the pension fund even further. It was a hard lesson learned by many.

Looking back, as sad as this entire Nortel situation was, it was a major life lesson for many of us in the financial planning profession: You can't always assume that things will work out the way you think they will, and you can't simply rely on employment pensions and benefits in your planning. As much as we might like to think that pensions are inviolate and that big companies can't fail, the fall of one of Canada's most famous companies and the 2008–09 financial crisis are strong reminders of one of the most basic of financial planning adages: Don't put all your eggs in one basket.

Even if spending time thinking about money is not your thing, make sure you take the time to check out your company's pension and benefit plans each year. Don't be afraid to ask some hard questions, and if your employer is in tight financial times, find a qualified professional to help you dig a bit deeper, so you understand the risks to you.

20

A Values-driven Approach to Growing Wealth

W hen we started working with Molly, she was in a tough place. Her marriage had ended suddenly, and she was left looking at a very different future as a single mom. She gave me a call and said she wanted to take a long, hard look at her financial plans and how things would change for her going forward in her new circumstances.

Molly's case was really fascinating — given her relatively young age, she had done an amazing job of saving. She had just taken over a business, and things were going well. The good news was, she and her ex had done great planning work, and she and her child were going to be OK. She just needed some help to see this in order to put her mind to rest.

I've learned over the years that any good financial plan ideally starts with a good discussion about personal values. When Molly and I met to discuss her new situation, we could really focus on just her, and that was when I learned that she is a hardcore environmentalist. Not only did she support a number of nature trusts and charities, she was an active volunteer and even went so far as to wash out and reuse resealable sandwich bags to keep plastic out of the garbage. Turns out, almost every decision Molly made in her personal life was done with environmental considerations in mind.

A Big Disconnect

Fast-forward to a week or so later. One of the main points of doing a financial plan is to look at one's investments and see how they are structured. As I went through the analysis, I started to realize that a large chunk of Molly's investment holdings, almost 40 percent, were in . . . wait for it . . . the Alberta oil sands! At the time, oil stocks were riding high, and her portfolio had done very well as a result, so I could understand why her stockbroker might have chosen to put her in these investments. I was baffled, however, that she would have knowingly agreed to this, as it was a fundamental breach of her strongest personal values.

When I came back to her with her planning report, her eyes widened. Then, she became really, really angry. Her stockbroker had known that she was donating to several environmental charities — in fact, she had been making gifts of publicly traded securities to fund her donations. (The CRA gives an extra tax break on in-kind charitable gifts of publicly traded securities on top of the normal donation credit.)

"Oh my god," she said to me. "I've been prioritizing returns over what I believe in. I feel awful."

Helping Molly Align Her Portfolio with Her Principles

One of my suggestions was that Molly shift a pile of her holdings into socially responsible investments (SRI) and, in particular, some that specialized in minimizing the carbon footprint of her holdings. We were able to find a portfolio structure that took her from 40 percent investment in the oil sands, to less than 7 percent of her Canadian holdings in fossil fuels, and none at all in the global part of her portfolio. Interestingly, the history of the funds was such that she wouldn't actually have had to give up any returns over the same time period; the more environmentally friendly portfolio I recommended would have actually outperformed her oil-sands-laden portfolio.

SRI funds adhere to a variety of investing principles, but in general, they all have a mandate to invest only in ethical businesses. The concept of ethical business varies from person to person and culture to culture, so different funds exist to meet different needs. As a group, however, SRI funds tend to have a more activist investment philosophy to effect positive change, as well as a tendency to look at more than just a bottom line return as a valuation method.

Today, Molly sleeps a lot easier knowing that her retirement savings plans are in alignment with her values. A recent report on her investments showed her Canadian holdings have a carbon footprint that is 64 percent lower than a typical Canadian equity portfolio, and her international investments are even better at a carbon footprint of 23 percent of the average international portfolio in Canada. For someone who values the environment as much as Molly does, SRI funds are a great fit. Those numbers sure help her breathe easier, in every way you can imagine.

Your value system might look like Molly's, or maybe it's completely different and unique to you. We are fortunate enough to live in a time where you can — and should — be able to match your personal values and your investment values very closely. Beyond that, a recent analysis of investment holdings here in Canada strongly suggests that SRI funds might be good for your pocketbook. In the five-year period ending in May of 2019, returns for SRI funds in Canada outpaced non-SRI funds in every single category. That's an impressive track record — and the analysts I've talked to on the subject suspect that the extra level of investigation done by SRI managers into the ethics of companies they invest in is a factor in this superior performance. Time will tell if this trend holds up, but the logic seems sound to me. And it sure sounds good to Molly, who is sleeping much better at night knowing she hasn't compromised her value system, nor has she sacrificed investment performance for her principles.

Today, Molly is thriving personally and professionally and moving on with life. She's still washing out those plastic sandwich bags, though — because that's just who she is.

21

Five Easy Ways to Destroy Your Wealth

Believe it or not, I'm an optimist — but sometimes it's good to look at the dark side to figure out how not to end up in a bad place! As a financial planning professional, I aim to help clients not only to accomplish their ambitious financial goals and retirement dreams, but also to plan for contingencies and bumps along the way. With good planning, we can even avoid worst-case scenarios. In my practice, I see people making the same mistakes year in and year out, and I hope that sharing them with you here will help you avoid them. Following are the five most common ways in which people destroy their wealth.

1. Accumulating Too Much in Your RRSP/RRIF

It sounds wrong, but one of the biggest tax traps in Canada lies in wait for those who are too good at saving. Due to quirks of the income tax rules, having too much money in your Registered Income Fund (RRIF) or Registered Retirement Savings Plan (RRSP) in your later years can come back to bite you.

Most commonly, chronic savers end up with their estate falling into the highest tax bracket (53.5 percent in my home province of Ontario) because every dollar in your RRIF or RRSP is counted in your income in your year of death. Although you can roll your own RRSP or RRIF over to your spouse tax-free at your death, that's only deferring the tax problem; if your spouse survives you, the Canada Revenue Agency (CRA) will eventually come calling to claim the full tax bill from your spouse's estate. Ironically, I often see scenarios whereby the tax bill generated by the value of the estate on the death of the second spouse is substantially higher than the taxes saved in the first place by both spouses' contributions to RRSPs over many years.

The second RRSP/RRIF tax trap happens at the time of the first spouse's death. The surviving spouse often finds himself or herself thrown into Old Age Security clawback status, losing some or all of the government benefit they're entitled to because their income is now too high. Anyone collecting OAS who is making over $77,580 in 2020 in annual net income loses fifteen cents for every dollar of net income over the threshold, until the benefit is entirely lost if you are making over $125,696. If your spouse dies and rolls his or her RRIF over to you tax-free, your minimum annual RRIF withdrawal will then be based on the higher combined total, potentially pushing your income over the clawback threshold and lowering, or eliminating, the amount of your OAS pension. This can come as a nasty surprise for folks who, when their spouse was alive, were able to income split and stay well below this threshold.

If you've amassed substantial assets in your RRSPs/RRIFs, consider using excess RRSP funds to make charitable contributions. If you don't need all the money you've saved in your RRSP to live on, this technique helps drain the RRSP over time in a tax-effective way. (Refer to Chapter 26, "The Most Fun I Have Ever Had Building a Financial Plan," for a great example of this strategy.)

A second opportunity is to prioritize maximizing your TFSA over your RRSP at a younger age. According to the CRA, the TFSA and RRSP are designed to be mathematically equal vehicles for long-term savings as far as taxation is concerned. However, at the moment, the OAS clawback threshold is not affected by your TFSA savings. I suspect this may change in the future, but it does — at the time of writing this book — tip the scales toward TFSAs being a better retirement-savings vehicle for some people.

2. Designating the Kids as Joint Owners of Assets to Avoid Probate

Fifteen years ago, I worked with clients whose mom had, after a conversation at her bridge game, decided it was a good idea to register her house jointly with her kids to avoid paying probate fees if they inherited the house on her death. But fifteen years later, Toronto real estate prices had climbed astronomically and Mom decided to sell the house (which would have been exempt from capital gains tax as her principal residence) for a tidy profit. The family was shocked to find out that this resulted in capital gains assessments to her two children who did not live in the house. The net result was $75,000 in income tax between the two kids. All this to save $1,800 in probate fees!

Never put someone on the title on your primary residence unless they live there, too. For you, your home is tax-exempt; for them, it's a secondary property and subject to capital gains tax. Similar issues can arise if you hold your non-registered assets, like Guaranteed Investment Certificates (GICs) and bank accounts, jointly with your children. While this can sometimes work, it can also create issues. First, changing the ownership of non-registered assets can trigger a disposition for tax purposes. Second, a number of Supreme Court rulings over the past ten years have made this a bit of a legal "grey area" for estate purposes. Thirdly, adding someone else on title (be it real estate or investments) might make the asset subject to seizure if the joint owner is sued, or owes money. There are other, better ways to accomplish the same outcome that don't come with the inherent risks of joint ownership.

If it's a house, it's almost always best if only the people who reside in the house are on the title. Non-registered accounts are often better handled through the use of an insurance-based GIC or a segregated fund, where a beneficiary is named. These products, unlike their non-insurance equivalents, will bypass probate without any of the legal grey areas of joint tenancy.

3. Trying to Make a Fast Buck with a Hot Stock Tip

For whatever reason, human nature is often driven by the fear of missing out (FOMO). As you have likely seen, marijuana stocks and cryptocurrencies have been dominating news headlines for the last few years. Some people made a pile of quick and "easy" money on these opportunities and started telling their friends. More recently, many people have been wiped out as the valuations on these "investments" have had huge downswings.

I have a hard time understanding how a company with no sales can be valued higher than the largest breweries in the world, or how a currency created by computer can be considered more valuable than those backed by governments.

Don't go there. Seriously. If you still feel the urge to invest in the latest trend, go buy a copy of Niall Ferguson's book, *The Ascent of Money: A Financial History of the World*, which is an engaging read through nearly 1,500 years of financial market history and covers other "hot tips" in earlier time periods, such as the great "tulip bubble" of the 1600s. You will learn very quickly that the human race has had centuries of hot tips leading to nasty results!

4. Waiting Too Long to Implement Smart Estate Strategies

There are many reasons people put off estate planning, but procrastination on this front usually comes with a large cost. With a long enough timeframe, you can take advantage of several strategies to save your estate a pile of taxes.

One key timeframe for making adjustments to your estate plan (or putting one in place, if you haven't already) is when you are in the age range of sixty to sixty-five. Many people have significant assets at this point in life, and much of the value is tied up in RRIFs or RRSPs. As you might recall from point number-one above, this is not necessarily ideal. Since OAS (and OAS clawback) kicks in at age sixty-five, and you *must* start withdrawals from your RRIF at age seventy-two, it's possible for us to reduce your RRSP holdings gradually between sixty and sixty-five with minimal tax implications. If your RRSP/RRIF is large by age seventy-two, your marginal tax rate may jump significantly when you start mandatory minimum withdrawals from your RRIF, counteracting the benefits of all your years of saving.

Additionally, we can use insurance to help offset the taxes due on your estate upon your death, either directly by naming your heirs as beneficiaries of the tax-free payout, or indirectly by naming a charity and having the estate use the tax receipt generated at the time of death. Ideally, you should set this kind of policy up between ages forty and sixty. While this strategy is still feasible later in life, often the costs and potential health issues make this far more costly than starting while young. People often view insurance premiums as an expense, not a smart investment in the future. Done right, these strategies can leave your family in a significantly improved financial position once you're gone.

Start working with an advisor on your estate planning as soon as possible and don't procrastinate. Every year you wait makes it slightly more difficult as your options become limited.

5. Divorce

Alas, the greatest destroyer of wealth we see is divorce. No matter your age, the emotional and financial costs associated with divorce take a heavy toll. Aside from the cautionary adage of "choose your spouse well" to avoid the whole mess entirely, the best you can do if you do find yourself in a divorce situation is to mitigate the costs.

Collaborative divorce is a growing trend, and we have seen it rising in popularity. The collaborative divorce process is designed to lead to more positive financial outcomes than the traditional method, by attempting to bypass the litigation often involved in divorce. This leads to (hopefully) lower legal costs. At the heart of the process is the concept that both parties agree to aim for the best mutually beneficial outcome, rather than favouring one side over the other. In Ontario, more information can be found at www.oclf.ca. While much of the information on the website is useful Canada-wide, you may find similar organizations in other provinces as the practice of collaborative divorce spreads across the country.

Get Good Advice to Be Successful

If there is a common thread among all five of the top eroders of wealth, it's that each scenario is often a result of blindly following a path that one believes to be true. Sound advice from properly qualified professionals will be worth its weight in gold for situations that you can't avoid or couldn't foresee yourself. Seek out professional advisors as early as you can, before you start making your own mistakes or find yourself in too deep. Of course, there is a cost to working with professionals, but great advice will save you far more money in the long run than you will pay for it.

22

When Your Brain Won't Let You Retire

"Alas for all those that never sing, but die with all their music in them."

—*Oliver Wendell Holmes*

Acolleague of mine, Adam, and I were talking one day over coffee about the psychology of retirement. Like myself, Adam found himself drawn to the financial planning business from a non-traditional (that is, non-business) background. Both of us had spent a large amount of time working on psychology courses in university, and we have both often found that having a psychological skill set is far more important for the work we do than having one in business or finance.

Through a curious coincidence, Adam and I discovered that we were each having the same kind of problem with a client approaching retirement. My client, François, was more than able to retire, wanted to retire, but couldn't bring himself to do so. Adam was having the exact same issue with his client, Henry.

Both Henry and François led weirdly parallel lives: Successful in their careers, they had been chronic savers their entire lives. Both were proud that they had the discipline through their later working years to save $1,000 a month, come hell or high water, no matter what. They had each been doing that for ten to fifteen years before retirement. I was frustrated, because as much as I could provide proof to François that he could retire, he couldn't get it out of his head that he would have to continue to save $1,000 a month in retirement as well. Adam was in the same boat with Henry.

Over drinks, Adam and I came up with a brilliant plan. We would set up a savings account for each of these two clients, and we would draw down funds monthly from the original retire-ment savings account and simply transfer them over to the new account. In essence, nothing would really change, other than that François and Henry would be able to feel as if they were "saving" each month. In reality, of course, nothing was really any different in their financial plans. The money was just moving between ac-counts. Once you retire, you generally start drawing down on, and living off of, the money you've been saving for years—not putting it away for your eventual demise!

It worked like a charm. Both François and Henry went into retirement feeling that they were still saving money. About eigh-teen months in, François turned to me in a meeting and said, "You know, it just dawned on me, this is kind of silly, isn't it? I guess I don't need to save money now that I am retired." We closed the "savings" account and transferred everything back to the original account, secure in the knowledge that our simple strategy had helped him safely transition to retirement with less stress.

This Is Your Brain on Work . . . and This Is Your Brain on Retirement

My colleague Adam often talks about the importance of changing your mindset as you approach retirement. We have so many habits that guide us that have been deeply ingrained over many years; it can be very hard to break them, and sometimes we don't even realize we are driven by them.

Adam shared another great story with me about his clients Maria and José. All their lives, Maria and José had dreamed of taking a trip to Scandinavia. They tucked money away at every opportunity and retired recently with a nice nest egg. Yet, when it came time to travel, which trip do you think they chose to go on? The one that was cheap, or their dream-of-a-lifetime trip?

Well, as you might suppose, they chose the cheapest trip. Which is fine, except that they had more than enough funds to enjoy the trip they dreamed of. When they got back, Adam worked hard to show them that their Scandinavian adventure was well within their means, but they would first need to give up their pre-retirement mindset of scarcity (giving things up to save for the future), now that they had capacity in retirement to use their savings and live the life they'd envisioned.

The next year, Maria and José went on their dream trip and

had an amazing time, thanks to Adam's advice and encouragement, which had helped to change their mindset. It was everything they hoped, and more, which just goes to show you that you can't always listen to the little voice in your head!

Often, we get trapped into thinking that growing our wealth only has to do with making the size of our portfolio bigger. However, enjoying true wealth is not just about money, but experience as well. Maria and José learned from Adam that part of their legacy grew from the joy of completing a big item on their bucket list, even if it meant emptying a bit from their retirement bucket.

Part 4

Creating a Legacy of Philanthropy

Once you have ensured that you've grown and protected your wealth, and you have been able to build a legacy that allows you and your family to be taken care of, it's time to start thinking about how you can leave a broader legacy to help others and the world around you. Including philanthropy and charitable giving in their estate plans is a high priority for many of our clients, but I find that most people have many questions and concerns about how best to accomplish this goal. People are always amazed to learn how many wonderful ways there are to make an impact on the world around us that is much, much bigger than we ever imagine possible. If you are similarly driven by purpose, then you're bound to be inspired by the stories in this section and feel motivated to start creating your own philanthropic legacy.

23

Birds of a Feather
Supporting the Right Kind of Charitable Organization for You

One of my pastimes is photography; in particular, bird and wildlife photography. We are very fortunate in London, Ontario, to live in a part of the world that lies on one of the major North American flyways. While most people in this part of Canada think of Point Pelee National Park in the spring for songbirds, or Aylmer for Tundra Swans, one of the coolest migrations is the hawk and raptor migration, which repeats every fall when over thirty-six thousand magnificent birds of prey fly over Hawk Cliff, just east of Port Stanley on the Lake Erie shoreline.

If you go, you will also be witness to two environmentally sensitive properties in very close proximity, both owned by charities.

One is the Hawk Cliff Woods,[32] owned by the Thames Talbot Land Trust (TTLT), a public land-trust foundation. Its purchase of the property was partly funded by the Ontario Trillium Foundation, an agency of the province that is run as a public foundation. The second property is Solitude Nature Reserve,[33] operated by a private foundation. Each of these organizations is doing some fantastic work in preserving the unique natural areas around Hawk Cliff; however, they go about it in very different ways, representing two excellent, but distinctive, approaches to philanthropy and legacy.

Private Foundation, Public Foundation, or Charity?

We typically use the word "charity" very broadly to include any organization that is doing good work for any cause; but, in fact, many different kinds of organizations fall under this umbrella. Technically, charitable organizations are specifically defined by the Canada Revenue Agency, and to qualify as a charity, the organization must be involved in at least one of the following:

- the relief of poverty,[34]
- the advancement of education,
- the advancement of religion, and/or

---

32 www.thamestalbotlandtrust.ca/hawkcliffwoods

33 www.solitudenaturereserve.com

34 One of the truly mind-boggling things in Canadian law is that prevention of poverty is not a charitable act — only its relief is!

- certain other purposes that benefit the community in such a way that courts have deemed charitable.

The last category is broad, but specific, and fortunately it includes the preservation of nature, allowing the Thames Talbot Land Trust to continue their good work at Hawk Cliff and elsewhere. Like foundations, charities must disburse at least 3.5 percent of their assets annually toward their charitable mandate. In the case of a land trust, this is easily met by working to preserve their properties and by purchasing new sensitive areas for future preservation.

Charities like the TTLT are run by a board of directors and have an operational purpose, or mission, that has a charitable mandate. In the case of TTLT, the mandate of the organization is to preserve environmentally sensitive land and protect wildlife along the Thames River and the Talbot Trail.

Private Foundations

A private foundation is another type of organization that does charitable work and, again, is defined very specifically by law. Private foundations are run by a closely held group, whereby 50 percent or more of the charity's directors are related by blood, adoption, or other means, such as mutually owning a business together. The CRA makes this distinction to ensure that a donor cannot exert too much control on assets they have donated, as one of the guiding principals of our charitable law is that in order to obtain a tax receipt, you must surrender control of the asset. If too many closely related people run a charity, the CRA puts special provisions in place to limit certain activities and types of donations. These restrictions are designed to prevent wealthy business owners or families from moving assets to charity as a tax strategy, without truly relinquishing control of them. The CRA believes that when a majority of the directors are not at arm's length, they could vote as a block and effectively still control donated assets.

While private foundations are driven by the philanthropic goals of the founders, the creation of these foundations is often timed as part of a tax-planning strategy for the sale of a business, as the sale may generate a significant tax bill to the owners. A private foundation is a very useful structure that allows you to generate an immediate tax credit and then disburse the funds to charity at a later date or over time, allowing the business owner time to determine charitable goals, mandates, and other issues at a later date.

Due to the close control of this type of charity, usually by the originator and his or her family, the CRA puts some restrictions on what types of gifts can be donated compared to other charities, and it demands slightly different reporting from them. As an example, private foundations have extra restrictions and conditions around gifts of private company shares, and they are forbidden from engaging in any business-type activity. They are also forbidden from running fundraising events, such as golf tournaments, charity runs, or other similar activities.

Public Foundations

Unlike private foundations, public foundations have a group of unrelated directors and, thus, have far fewer restrictions — including the ability to do fundraising events as well as run business operations. They otherwise operate in the same way. A public foundation, like the Ontario Trillium Foundation (OTF), is governed by an independent board of directors who are all at arm's length. OTF is actually a government agency of the province and is funded exclusively by it, making it different than most public foundations, which receive their funding from a number of diverse sources. However, in principle, the OTF operates in many of the same ways as any other public foundation, even though it has only one donor. Public foundations grant money to any number of charities. Like all charitable entities, they must disburse at least 3.5 percent of their holdings a year to maintain their tax status.

Bear in mind that, be it public or private, just because a charity has "foundation" in its name, doesn't actually mean it is a foundation according to CRA rules. Foundations generally are grant-providers to other charities and are not involved in operational capacities like registered charities. Typically, they flow funds through to charitable organizations that actually undertake a specific charitable mandate and do the work. For example, you might see a foundation exist to distribute funds to organizations that alleviate poverty and hunger, perhaps by providing funding to soup kitchens but not actually running a soup kitchen of its own.

An "In-Between" Solution: Donor-Advised Accounts

Recently, some public foundations have begun offering "donor-directed" or "donor-advised fund" accounts, designed to provide the best of both worlds for families and individuals who wish to commit to philanthropy over an extended period of time but who would prefer not to go to the trouble and expense of establishing a separate charitable structure of their own, with its own board and administrative overhead.

Donor-advised or donor-directed funds fall under the general provisions of a public foundation, but they permit each donor, and his or her appointed successors, to advise the public foundation on where they wish their annual disbursements to go. Provided that the charitable beneficiaries chosen by the individual donor meet the legal requirements necessary, the public foundation will forward the donor's funds to that specific charity.

Technically, the advice that donors give to the foundation about their accounts is just that — advice — and is not legally enforceable by the donor. On a practical basis, there are very few circumstances in which the donor's advice would not be followed; however, it is important to realize that there is legally less control in these accounts than there would be in a private foundation, where the donor can be a director with voting rights and be a key decision-maker. For a large number of donors, though, the donor-advised solution gives 99 percent of the benefits of the private foundation, with vastly less administrative burden and fewer headaches.

How About You?

All of these charitable structures provide our society with excellent benefits, such as the nature-preservation efforts around Hawk Cliff, which are supported by both public and private foundations. Most Canadians are likely to donate to a registered charity in their lifetime, but it is always wise to know there are multiple organizational structures you can access to make a major impact in your community.

Each species of charitable structure is governed by different rules and each presents different advantages and disadvantages, but all of them can help you accomplish your philanthropic vision. As with our avian friends, diversity of species is an important factor in the health of the charitable sector.

24

Holy
Expenses,
Batman!

O ne of the great joys of my professional life is doing
speaking engagements for donors to various charities
on the importance of giving and how to make giving
as effective as possible. I've presented to the donor base of major
national organizations as well as smaller local organizations, and
every time, people are surprised at how easy and effective it can be
to give. Most people don't know you can donate gifts of stock or
funds from your non-registered investment accounts and get an
extra tax break, and many business owners aren't aware of the myr-
iad ways they can give through their companies at a very low cost.

After these talks, I usually give an hour of my time to allow
for detailed answers to donors' questions specific to their financial
situation. Recently, Martha and Tom came to me after one such

talk. Martha and Tom, like many others, had been chronic savers in their RRSPs, and I was able to show them how to cut back dramatically on the taxes that would be due on their estate as a result. The majority of their investment holdings were going to be subject to 53.5 percent tax upon their death without some tax-planning strategies in place. In the process of this review, one of the most common questions I hear came up: "I'm worried that the charity we've chosen to support is spending too much on administrative costs and overhead."

I get this question a lot, and I think it's for two reasons. The first is thanks to the media, who seem to run endless stories, over and over, with examples of charities that incur high costs and that don't appear to be spending sufficiently on their mandate. The second reason, I think, is reflective of the type of people I tend to work with — frugal savers. Most of the folks we see have done a great job at saving, and they've done it by managing their expenses carefully. So, in light of this, for folks like Martha and Tom, I think the question is a natural one — if you have worked hard and saved your whole life, you don't want to risk having someone else treat your dollar less carefully than you do.

What Is a Reasonable Amount for a Charity to Spend on Overhead Costs?

There is, unfortunately, no straight answer to this question, other than, "It depends." As you might imagine, a larger charity likely will have higher overhead costs — and this usually is a good thing.

Would you want to support a charity that failed to carry insurance or that didn't have clear human resources policies? Would it be OK for a health-related charity to purchase a cheaper MRI machine that is not as safe as a more expensive model?

Smaller organizations are often hugely volunteer-driven and can run with minimal overheads. However, as they evolve, like any business, it's going to be necessary to spend money to make money. Any charity that claims that 99 percent of your donations goes directly to its cause is likely lying, or massively under-resourced.

You also have to take into account the type of charity. A foundation that disburses grants to support other charitable organizations should have much lower overhead and administrative costs than one that provides active services or has a "hands-on mandate," like a soup kitchen. Charities that provide humanitarian relief (like Doctors Without Borders, for example) probably have vastly higher costs relative to fundraising dollars than a small regional museum.

Making the Right Comparisons

One of the best ways for you to evaluate a charity is to compare it to its closest peers. One way you can do that is via the Canada Revenue Agency's charity directory.[35] Here, you can find all kinds of information, including the last five years of the organization's charitable tax returns.

There are numerous outside agencies that claim to rate

---

35 https://apps.cra-arc.gc.ca/ebci/hacc/srch/pub/dsplyBscSrch?request_locale=en

charities; however, frankly, I am highly skeptical of most of them. Most of these organizations run a numerical analysis of the different charities and make assumptions about what numbers each organization should have. It's never that simple, and rarely do they take the time to dive down into each individual charity to investigate it across multiple years. So, for example, an organization that is investing heavily in future growth due to increasing demand might end up with a poor rating for its administrative expenses. Investing in growth is a wise investment; therefore, proactively spending money now is a good sign — not a bad one just because it made that year's expenses higher. Context is everything, and I have yet to see an "outside agency" analysis put much into context.

The very best way to understand an organization is to volunteer for it and spend some time "living in its world." You'll learn more by being actively engaged with it than through any other method. Something else you can do is take a look on the CRA directory at the numbers for your favourite charity, and then compare them to the results for similar organizations. If you look at the "Quick View" section, you can see the percentage the charity is spending on management and administration.

In my opinion, most charities of similar size and scope should all have about the same overhead costs. If you notice that a particular charity has substantially higher expenses, it might be a warning sign. Even more worrying to me, however, is a charity whose overhead costs are substantially lower than its peers on a regular basis — this may be an indication that they are skimping on important items. If you take the time to get to know the charity and look at its financial history, you'll be best positioned to ask the right (and sometimes tough) questions.

One Last Thought

To underscore the importance of putting the question about charity expenses in context, I will leave you with the same thoughts that I left with Martha and Tom. In general terms across all types of organizations, charities who can keep the cost to raise a dollar below 25 percent are usually considered to be doing an excellent job. If you stop to think about it, this means that the charity is raising $3 for every $1 of cost, which is a profit margin of 300 percent above expenses in business terms. By any standard, that is exceptional; in the world of private business, a sustained profit margin of 30 percent would be considered wildly successful for many industries. By that measure, charities on the whole are a roaring success.

Donors like Martha and Tom are justified in asking questions regarding charity expenses — but in almost every case, their favourite organizations, and yours, are extraordinarily efficient and deserving of our support. And, at the end of the day, isn't the most important question about the management of any charity whether they are actively fulfilling their mandate? Empowering yourself to learn how to ask the right questions, like Martha and Tom did, will help you determine how comfortable you are with your donation.

25

Just
How Long
Is Forever?

I love all things space-related. I spend my nights taking photos of space from my backyard. In addition to my inherently nerdy nature (which comes as little shock to those who know me), I've been a lifelong insomniac, photographer, and nature lover — so, stargazing seemed like the perfect hobby to take up.

Taking pictures of the universe involves all kinds of measurements of time. When we take pictures of objects in our solar system — like the moon, sun, and planets — we use cameras that take high-speed video, with each exposure being only a few milliseconds. When we want to take pictures of very faint, distant objects in deep space, we take many long exposures to create a picture that might have ten or twenty hours of exposure time. That's a lot of time, but it pales in comparison to how long it took the light of the stars to reach my camera's sensor. To help you understand how vast and empty space is: it takes 4.2 years for the light from our nearest neighbouring star to reach us!

But what's truly mind-blowing is that the light from distant galaxies takes millions of years to reach us. The Whirlpool Galaxy is estimated to be far enough away from us that it takes 23.16 million years for its light to arrive here. And, as luck would have it, it's one of our closest neighbouring galaxies in the universe. Thanks to the Hubble Space Telescope, we know of many galaxies so far away that it took their light five billion years to reach us.

That's a long, long time. Strangely, one area of financial and estate planning that is often underestimated is the passage of time and its effects on your planning. Many people wish to create a legacy that will last "forever," but they don't really understand just what that actually means, and how restrictive it can be.

Be Careful How You Define "Forever" in Your Will

I've encountered many folks who want to give a gift to charity by way of endowment. An endowment allows you to leave a sum of money that will generate interest to provide ongoing, long-term funding to a charity, potentially forever. It's a great idea and an incredibly generous gift. However, as one local charity I recently worked with discovered, the nature of time can rear its ugly head.[36]

---

36 I am, of course, referring to their gift. A similar experience happens to me every time I look in the mirror in the morning, but that is an entirely different issue.

A number of donors had left the charity endowments of $1,000 or $5,000, sums that fifty or one hundred years ago seemed like a lot of money; however, inflation having taken its toll, today these gifts are relatively small. And with our low interest rate environment (of around 2 percent at the time of writing), it's easy to see that the $20 or $100 in interest generated each year from these gifts wasn't doing much good for anyone. It also didn't help that the program these gifts were supposed to support no longer existed.

There are many other programs run by this particular charity where a lump sum of $1,000 or $5,000 would make an impact. But unfortunately, from a legal perspective, once a charity accepts a gift, the terms of the gift can't ever be changed. In this case, there was no clause in the original gift agreements to let the charity re-direct the funds. The only option for the charity was to go to a judge and ask for permission to change the purpose of the funds. This was a costly procedure in terms of both time and money.

Part of the problem is that an endowment is intended to last in perpetuity, and perpetuity is a very long time. In the words of lawyer Terry Carter (a fellow member of the Canadian Association of Gift Planners and one of the most knowledgeable people on this topic I've ever met), the definition of perpetuity is longer than a human life, longer than the charity will exist, longer than human existence will last, longer than our sun will last, and even longer than our galaxy will exist — it's for the lifetime of the universe. Endowment isn't a word to be used lightly when making a gift, either via your will or in your lifetime.

So, What Can You Do?

There are other ways to donate generously that allow more flexibility. For example, you could negotiate with the charity to ensure your gift is fully spent over a more reasonable time period of, say, ten years. Or, you can look at donor-directed or donor-advised fund options offered by some charitable foundations, which give you more flexibility to make changes to the purpose of the funds after the initial point of donation. Either of these options would have saved our friends at the charity in our example a lot of wasted expense and time, had they been in place for these fifty-year-old donations!

Like all aspects of your financial and estate plans, structuring charitable gifts most effectively takes some thought, including understanding what works best for the charity receiving the funds. Make sure you bring in the right expert to make this work. And remember that smart planning will put you over the moon, but bad planning will get you and your estate thrown into the sun.[37]

---

37 This summer, I hope you'll take time to get out of the city to where the sky is dark, look up, enjoy the amazing universe above us, and contemplate the nature of eternity, like I do. It's a treasure we're slowly losing to light pollution from our urban areas. For more information on Canada's dark-sky preserves, you can investigate the Royal Astronomical Society of Canada's website at www.rasc.ca/dark-sky-site-designations.

26

The Most Fun I Have Ever Had Building a Financial Plan

I n early December 2016, I probably had the most fun I've ever had working with a client. Joan (or so we will call her to protect the innocent) is in her late fifties, recently retired, and a chronic saver. She had realized that her chronic savings habits had placed her in a bit of a pickle: between her and her husband, Ted, they had nearly $700,000 tucked away in RRSPs (Registered Retirement Savings Plans) and LIRAs (Locked-In Retirement Accounts), and at some point, these funds were going to be taxed heavily when they started drawing on them for retirement income, and even more so if any funds were left over in their estate. However, because Joan and Ted have a very modest lifestyle, they were quite comfortable living on Ted's pension and their income from a bit of casual work they both did in retirement. Therefore, they really didn't think they would need the income from those RRSPs and LIRAs after all those years of socking the money away.

When we looked at the tax situation from an estate-planning point of view, it quickly became clear that the government would end up taking nearly 50 percent of the $700,000 in RRSPs if we did nothing. The tax bill on their estate if they both died today would be around $300,000 and, based on our projections, would likely climb to $500,000 if their portfolio continued to grow in value and they lived into their mid-seventies!

Needless to say, Joan was rather aghast at the situation, especially because she was paying very little in tax at the time. Her income would continue to be quite small (around $25,000 a year) until her OAS and CPP kicked in at age sixty-five, and then it would jump significantly when she would be forced to start withdrawing from her RRSPs/RRIFs at age seventy-two.

Fortunately, Joan is very, very interested in philanthropy. We realized that because of her low income, she could pull money from her RRSP right away at a tax rate of about 20 percent, which is way better than the 53.5 percent maximum rate Joan and Ted's estate would be subject to in Ontario on most of their RRSPs. This is also much lower than her tax rate will be in her sixties and seventies when she starts collecting her government pensions and must start withdrawing from her RRIFs.

Step 1: Drain the RRSP, Give Money to Charity

Today, while her income remains low and she is in a 20 percent tax bracket, Joan is going to pull $12,000 a year from her RRSP for ten years and donate that amount to charity. That donation entitles her to a tax break of roughly 40 percent here in Ontario. Half of the donation credit of 40 percent will pay the tax on the withdrawal. The other half lets her pull out approximately another $10,000 a year from her RRSP — essentially tax-free due to the charitable tax credit — and turn around and re-invest it in the TFSAs (Tax-Free Savings Accounts) belonging to her and Ted. At the end of ten years, they will have accumulated about $125,000 in their TFSA accounts (assuming they get a 4 percent return on their money) and none of it will be subject to tax.

By the time she's started collecting CPP and OAS at age sixty-five, Joan will have drained $220,000 from her RRSP and will have a net $125,000 in her pocket, leaving her virtually in the same financial position after ten years as had she left the money in the RRSP, but with a greatly reduced tax bill that is much lower than either later withdrawals or estate taxes would have incurred.

Step 2: Multiply the Effect — Big Time!

The really exciting part of this strategy is how we are going to handle the donation to the charity. Rather than just giving cash, we are setting up an insurance policy that will be owned by the charity and paid for by Joan's generous $12,000 annual gift. This policy will pay out $400,000 to the charity once both Joan and Ted have died. We are turning their $120,000 into $400,000 — multiplying their gift by more than 300 percent by using the insurance.[38]

The Net Result

After ten years of following the strategy outlined in the plan we developed, Joan will have the same amount of money in her estate, she will have reduced her income in her seventies (which is unneeded and would be heavily taxable then), and she will have managed to make a $400,000 gift to her favourite charity.

That's a $400,000 transformational gift made to charity at basically a net cost of near zero to her estate. This is a win-win for Joan and Ted and for their chosen charity. In addition to the tax and financial advantage this couple enjoys, the community-based charities that are near and dear to Joan's heart will receive some of their largest gifts ever as part of her and Ted's legacy.

Both Joan and I skipped all the way home with big smiles on our faces the day we finally implemented her plan. It remains to this day the most fun I've ever had at work, and it is a great example to all of us that we are capable of making a significant philanthropic impact at a much higher level than we might expect.

---

38 Ted and Joan are using a different strategy than Bridget and I used, which I describe in more detail later in Chapter 32. In their case, the insurance is owned by the charity, and in ours, the charity is simply the beneficiary. Bridget and I retain the flexibility to change the charities in the future, but we don't get a tax credit now for our premiums. Ted and Joan can't ever change the charity — but they get tax credits in their lifetime. You have to choose one method or the other. The CRA doesn't let you have your cake and eat it, too!

Part 5

My Own
Life and Legacy

I am a big believer in the importance of walking
the walk and not just talking the talk. I spend my
professional life talking about philanthropy, estate
planning, and financial planning, and I wouldn't be
doing any of it if I didn't believe it down to the very
core of my soul. I do my best to ensure that what I
do in my personal life and my own planning is also
driven by purpose, and I hope that sharing some of
my own stories will inspire you to plan and create
your legacy as well.

27

My Two Grannies

As a young man, I was very fortunate to have the friendship of two octogenarian ladies, Martha and Jane, who were like surrogate grandmothers to me. Having them in my life was a huge gift, because my own maternal grandmother and grandfather died when I was a young child. While I have many fond memories of my real grandmother, we had precious little time together.

I developed such a wonderful relationship with both Martha and Jane, I consider them my honorary grandmothers. Although the two ladies never met, they were both huge influences in my life, and I owe them a great deal. They had a major impact on how I view life, wealth, and money, as well as many other things.

Martha: A Wealth of Heart and Happiness

I had known Martha ever since I was born, and she was closely tied to our family. She had a wicked sense of humour, was an incredible cook — the best I have ever known — and had a heart that was as big as the universe. An immigrant like my grandparents, she came to Canada from what is now known as Slovakia, as a teenager in the 1930s. It was, as you can imagine, quite the culture shock. But, being a warm, social kind of gal, she made friends quickly. Despite this, life wasn't always easy, especially as her parents were adjusting to life in Canada.

One of my favourite stories of hers is about the time her friends at school showed her how to put on makeup. When she got home that night, excited to show what she had learned from her friends, her father made her wash it off with water from the toilet while he yelled at her, "No daughter of mine will go around like a painted whore!" To say there was a culture clash within her household would be putting it lightly!

Martha met the love of her life at a young age, and they married almost as soon as they met. Like her, her husband Arthur was warm, generous of spirit, and full of humour. Together they raised six kids, which was not an easy task in the post-war years. They never had much money. Arthur worked long, hard hours, but six little mouths to feed meant little money was left over each week. Tragically, Arthur died just before retirement, leaving few resources behind for the family.

Despite how little she had, Martha was always, always happy. In her words, though she had nothing financially, she had lots of love, a terrific family, and a healthy ability to laugh. Despite a very modest lifestyle, life was good for her. Martha lived to see her ninety-first birthday, despite some pretty hefty health issues that had plagued her since her forties. For her, money was not what brought happiness and fulfillment.

The last time I saw Martha, a month or two before she died, she talked about her sister, who had passed away a few years before at a much younger age. Her sister, Alice, had had lots of money, a great husband, a great job, and everything you could imagine. And yet, said Martha, Alice was never happy. No matter what she had, it was never enough. Martha was convinced that her sister died so young because she never appreciated that being happy was worth far more than being wealthy.

Jane: The Lady Who Worried If She Had Enough

My other "adopted" grandma was Jane. Jane was a force of nature, to say the least! She was a mover and shaker who got things done. She was active even into her late eighties, and the hardest worker I have ever known. She was a regular volunteer for at least three charitable organizations that I knew of. She would serve on a board as readily as she would volunteer to make sandwiches, wash windows, or whatever was needed to get things done. Jane had little patience for anyone who couldn't — or wouldn't — keep up to her frenetic pace.

Once, both she and I were volunteering on something time

sensitive, with a quickly approaching deadline. One of our colleagues — although a lovely, lovely man — was rather fond of hearing his own voice. Jane, mustering as much self-control as she could, turned to me and said, "If only he could move the rest of himself as fast as his jaw, we could have been done two hours ago!" You did not mess with Jane. And lord help you if you didn't want to work. She was a hoot to work with, but only if you could keep up!

In her late eighties, Jane's health took a turn for the worse and she developed cancer. Like everything else in her life, she dealt with it in a pragmatic, no-nonsense kind of way. One limitation that frustrated her to no end later in life was that she had never gotten a driver's licence. Her husband had always done the driving, but it wasn't really an issue until he passed away in his early eighties. "Ryan," she said to me once, "it's terrible. Because of my health I'm not comfortable on the bus, and every time I take a cab, it costs me $25 to do a round trip to the doctor, the grocery store, or the bank! I'm going to be destitute."

Her daughter, Leslie, pulled me aside shortly after and told me that Jane, a child of the Depression era, had so much money tucked away that she wouldn't even dent the interest payments if she took a cab ten times a day. Leslie pleaded with me to chat with her mom and try to convince her it wasn't the end of the world to spend the fortune she had saved in order to have a better quality of life in her last days.

Like Martha, Jane made it into her early nineties before succumbing to the cancer. I guarantee you she still probably tried to show up to volunteer somewhere the day after she died, and some angel probably got an earful on her arrival about work that needed doing. That's just the kind of lady she was, and I loved her dearly for it.

Too Much or Too Little? How Much Do You Need?

Martha's and Jane's outlook toward their wealth — or their perceived lack of it — taught me a lot about the importance of understanding how much you actually need to retire on. Martha had no money, but she didn't need money to live her life and love it. Her lifestyle costs were as close to zero as she could manage, and she was always content with what she had. Her mindset was one of abundance: making do with what she had and feeling that her life was rich because of her relationships. Jane, in contrast, had more than enough money but was scared to spend it. She could never dispel her fear of running out of funds. Even at age ninety and in failing health, when there was no risk that she would outlive her money, Jane's mindset was one of scarcity.

Financial planning is always a balancing act between these two extreme perspectives, and figuring out how much is enough for you is part of the trick to having peace of mind when it comes to your money. So, next time you are sitting down to look at your finances, please take a moment and remember the tale of my two wonderful adopted grannies. No matter what amount of wealth you have — you should still be able to live life to its fullest, and not in fear.

28

The Great Pumpkin

A Story about Mental Health

When my son was younger, he was absolutely obsessed with Charles Schultz's *Peanuts* comics. He can still tell you what date Sally first appeared in the comics, how Lucy was a baby at one point, and discuss when the *Peanuts* gang first appeared in a cancelled precursor comic called *Li'l Folks*. His life goal is to become an animator, and I'm pleased to say he's well on his way.

Like many other Canadian children, he faces some mental health issues — there is a genetic anxiety disorder that pops up in our family from time to time — and his obsessive-compulsive factual knowledge of Peanuts is one of the many results of his genetics. With the anxiety, there comes a tremendous gift. He sees everything differently than most people do, which can be just as much a blessing as it can be a curse. Most of the time, it makes him a brilliant, highly creative kid with a keen sense of humour.

Like many other Canadian parents, we're concerned about what the future holds for our son. After lots of hard work and therapy, we think he'll lead a very exciting and productive life, but we have to stop and think carefully about our estate plans — particularly what we can do to provide for him if things turn out differently for him.

Planning for Family Members with Special Needs

When it comes to estate planning, I cannot overstate the importance of making sure each of your professional advisors understands any and all special needs that are specific to your family. I recently met with a client whose lawyer had written a will incorporating what's known as a Henson trust. It was brilliant work, using this special kind of trust, which is designed to ensure that adult children who receive the Ontario Disability Support Program don't *overinherit* to the point where their government benefits and access to programs and services are taken away. It's a tricky aspect of estate planning, but also a very important one.

Unfortunately, in this case, the client's investment advisor wasn't aware of the child's special needs and had structured the family's investment portfolio in such a way that most of the family's assets would be transferred directly to the child and bypass the will. This meant the disabled adult child would inherit too much money directly and be immediately ineligible for crucial support programs. Obviously, this wasn't a good scenario, especially given that the family thought everything was in order from a legal point of view. In fact, the investment advisor's strategy was working in direct conflict with the one the lawyer had so carefully put in place to protect the clients' special-needs child.

Integrated planning is critical. Make sure your financial advisor, lawyer, accountant, and other professionals you work with are fully aware of your specific family situation and receive regular updates when anything changes.

Ensuring Adequate Support for Your Dependants Is Crucial

In Ontario and many other jurisdictions, your estate has a legal obligation to support anyone who is financially dependent on you, including disabled children. A court has the power to override any beneficiary designation on insurance policies, RRIF/RRSP assets, and your will if you fail to provide adequately for them. This can wreak havoc on tax planning if, for example, a charitable bequest is overridden by the court to flow money to the dependent beneficiary, therefore requiring the estate to pay significantly higher taxes than originally planned.

We often see this scenario unfold in other situations as well, when it comes to spousal support payments or failing to update a will after recognizing common-law status with a new partner, for example. Similar consequences can also occur when somebody who was providing support to elderly parents with limited resources dies.

If you fail to provide for your disabled dependants, the courts can make sure that they are taken care of despite any estate plans you may have carefully designed. Be sure to review your estate plans and ensure you make *all* your professional advisors aware of the special circumstances in your family, and discuss with them any life updates that impact your financial situation.

29

How My Mom's Death Made Me a Better Financial Planner

I've spent most of this book telling stories about other people, but this chapter is much more intimate and personal. In late 2012, my mom received the call from the doctor that everyone fears, and we learned that she had breast cancer. She had a lumpectomy, and the diagnosis turned out to be worse than thought; she was then told that she would need chemotherapy, as well as radiation.

If someone you love has gone through this, you know the full range of emotions and stress your family has to endure. It is one of the experiences that life sends your way to remind you what is truly important and what is just "noise."

Our family learned a lot of important things in the last few months my mom was alive. For the most part, these are not things that we talk much about when doing financial or estate planning, but they can be huge practical and emotional issues for any family experiencing something similar. Here are just a few of the many important things we learned on our journey through Mom's last days.

Finding Things Can Be Challenging

As the disease progressed, we suspected that the cancer may have spread to my mother's brain in her last few months at home, which led to some odd behaviour. In particular, she felt the need to move her wedding certificate, driver's licence, and other key documents to some very strange places. We needed the wedding certificate to transfer her CPP and pension plan assets to Dad. As it turned out, she had moved it to a drawer in the basement.[39] We spent hours looking for it, only to find it by accident.

We had an even harder time finding Mom's wedding ring. She took it off just before going into the hospice, and it actually took eight months before Dad finally found her ring! While in the bigger scheme of the estate, these seem like small issues, they can be very upsetting for a family dealing with the emotional distress of losing a loved one.

---

39 It was there along with underwear, socks, and some kitchenware. I'm not sure what Mom was thinking, but that drawer was incredibly tidy and organized, as if that were a perfectly logical combination of items to have in one place, in a random basement drawer.

Online-only Banking Is Suddenly Not So Convenient

Mom had a portion of her assets with an online-only bank, as she enjoyed the ability to manage her finances from her computer. After she passed away, we quickly learned that this relatively new type of financial institution did not seem prepared to handle estate issues. We were simply trying to transfer what was in her accounts over to Dad, but it quickly became incredibly frustrating.

After a month of persistent effort, $60 in registered mail, and a lot of time on hold, we were finally able to transfer her accounts. One of the biggest stumbling blocks was that we couldn't meet with any bank representatives in person, and we had to sit around and wait on hold or wait to be called back to get anything done. Bricks-and-mortar financial institutions can almost always settle these transfers in a matter of hours and with minimal hassle with an in-person visit. Meeting in person with a death certificate from a funeral home and other appropriate documentation in hand ensures that you can know immediately if any crucial information is missing.

Don't Wait Too Long to Set Up a POA

It's always wise to set up powers of attorney (POA) for property (to manage financial matters) and for personal care (to make health care decisions), but it's absolutely critical to do this quickly if a family member becomes ill. There is no telling when your loved one will become physically or cognitively incapable of handling their own affairs, and you need to be ready to step in if and when required. You also need to be provided with copies of these essential documents or at least know where they are when the time comes.

Before we had her original POAs in hand, Mom tried to get information on her credit card accounts over the phone. Unfortunately, due to the medications and other effects of her disease, she wasn't able to answer the security questions correctly and she hung up in frustration. This resulted in some late payments on her accounts because we had no way of knowing what the balances were. If we had had the POAs at the ready, we could have dealt with all this ourselves and spared her the aggravation.

Don't Rely Only on Technology for Important Documents

We dealt with a financial institution that is usually very good at handling situations in which POAs, wills, and executor documents are required. In managing Mom's affairs, they were typically helpful and efficient. However, when we had to access Mom's accounts from their branch nearest the hospice where Mom spent her last few weeks, the local branch was unable to find the POA details on their system. For whatever reason, that branch was unable to access the account records.

Even if your financial institution scans in copies of all the key legal documents, technology can fail you when you most need to rely on it. It's always best to have a paper copy when you need something done urgently. Fortunately, I had a separate notarized copy with me that day and was able to provide it as evidence that I was allowed to act on her behalf.

Save a List of Important Contacts

Mom kept in touch with many of her friends around the world via email. When she moved into the hospice, we brought her a laptop that we could also use to keep everyone up to date; however, her desktop computer had all her email contacts stored on it. As a result, we couldn't easily put her in touch with her friends unless they emailed her first. Additionally, the laptop did not have any of the saved passwords or account numbers for any of her financial affairs, and she became quite frustrated as her memory failed her while attempting to log on.

Shortly after her death, we realized that we didn't know all of Mom's passwords. There were some programs we could not access after she was gone, meaning that we were never able to retrieve contact information for some of her friends. That was a shame, as we had hoped to use that list to make sure we had contacted everyone to let them know Mom had gone.

Be Prepared for Some Strange Requests

In her last few weeks, Mom kept insisting she needed large quantities of cash on hand. The hospice (and our family) was very uncomfortable having a patient keep cash in the facility. Trust officer friends of mine confirmed that this is a situation they often encounter, and it is a surprisingly common end-of-life demand. Finding ways to deny Mom's repeated requests for cash, while maintaining dignity for all involved, was far trickier than we imagined — but it was very important to protect Mom, and to protect the hospice staff from any risk of liability. We dealt with it by deferral, telling her we would bring the funds the next day — and then "forget" to do so. That kept her unagitated, and, sadly, she would usually forget that she had made the request the day before. It was the best way to handle a very uncomfortable, and sometimes tense, situation.

Review Your Beneficiary Designations on a Regular Basis

Elsewhere in this book, I've talked about the importance of reviewing the beneficiary designations on your accounts on a regular basis so that your money does not go to the wrong person. Life circumstances can change suddenly and the beneficiary you named, say, three years ago may not be the person you want to inherit your life insurance, RSSP or RRIF assets, or pension money today.

My parents were pretty good at keeping up with that kind of stuff, but just four months before Mom died, we found one account that did not have a properly designated beneficiary. Fortunately, she still had the capacity to sign a beneficiary change form and could make it right in time. It's very important to note that the holder of the assets must make this change themselves — a Power of Attorney cannot alter beneficiary designations on their behalf.

You Don't Have to Go It Alone

Our family owes an *immense* debt of gratitude to the wonderful people at St. Joseph's Hospice in London, Ontario. I cannot imagine how we would have survived the last few months of Mom's life without their incredible compassion, expertise, and support.

If you have never experienced a residential hospice setting and you or a member of your family are terminally ill, I would strongly encourage you to reach out to your local hospice for a tour. Every single person I have ever met who had a loved one's final journey end in a hospice has had nothing but a wonderful experience. To me, hospice is the finest aspect of health care ever developed.

We're also grateful for the planning work we did in the last few years to minimize the difficulty of settling Mom's estate when the time finally came. Despite the challenges we faced as a family, we managed to settle 99.9 percent of her estate within a month after her passing. I'm extremely grateful for the wisdom gained from the many fine professionals in law, accounting, financial planning, banking, and trusts whom I've worked with over the years. Losing someone you love is heartbreaking, but with the right advice, planning, and support in place, dealing with such a devastating loss is made a little less difficult and a little more bearable.

30

Life
Goes On

As with a major loss in so many other families, my mom's passing is fuzzy in my memory now. A health crisis like cancer in the family means that you all do what you must to make it through the difficult times. But like all things, time heals all wounds.

That said, we had as many learning moments over the year or so after the fact as we did in the all the time my mom was ill. The effects on financial and estate plans last for several years, so there are always unresolved matters that need to be dealt with, which will continue to teach you a thing or two. Here are a few things we learned that I hope will help you in your own planning.

Your Tax Situation Can Be Worse as a Single Than as Part of a Couple

As my dad is discovering, from a tax perspective, a couple is often treated more favourably than a single in many ways. RRIF/RRSP rollovers to a spouse mean that in the year following the death of your partner, you can end up with GIS or OAS clawbacks, as you no longer have income-splitting opportunities, and your minimum RRIF withdrawal is now based on the combined assets of you and your spouse, which are now held in one account.

Needless to say, the January after Mom's passing brought a big surprise for Dad: the higher annual income he now has to pull from his RRIF, and the impact it will have on his taxes.

Give Yourself Time Before Making Big Decisions

I think it's safe to say that my dad, my sister, and I have been learning that, although one adjusts, the grieving process can take far longer to work through than you might anticipate. You may even find that it impairs your judgment at unexpected times. Generally, it's not wise to make big financial decisions for a year or so.

The mourning process takes time, and you may find that it affects you in funny ways. I still remember one of my strongest moments of grief hit me while driving on a business trip nearly two years after Mom's passing. A random thought crossed my mind and my first reaction was, "I should call Mom and see how she is doing." I teared up so much I had to pull over to the side of the road. It was a strong reminder that you may still be subconsciously grieving long after you think it's possible. That moment served to reinforce my belief that one should never make big financial or life decisions until a year or more has passed after the death of a loved one.

Time to See the Lawyer about Your Will and POAs

Generally speaking, if you are part of a couple, your lawyer should have written your wills to anticipate one spouse predeceasing the other. That said, my entire family now finds ourselves in a situation where we should all be revising our wills and powers of attorney. Some of the reasons are practical (Mom was named as one of my backup POAs), but others are more subtle.

Having witnessed the last three years of Mom's decline, we have all formed new opinions on what we would or wouldn't want if we find ourselves in a similar situation in the future. The directions I would give in my POA document today are very different from those I specified a few years ago.

On a more practical front, my father's will and POAs, and my own, reference my mother in a number of spots that are no longer relevant. It's probably best to remove those references to prevent any unanticipated lack of clarity going forward. I cannot overemphasize that any major life event should be a trigger to review these critical documents, and the death of someone so close and central to the family is no exception.

Charitable Giving Changes with the Death of a Loved One

I think it's fair to say that some folks in my family who traditionally haven't donated to charity a lot in their lifetime have begun to donate significant amounts for the first time. (A fact of which I am immensely proud, given my profession and specialty in charitable planning!)

Bridget and I have given generously to several causes over the years, and we've now included St. Joseph's Hospice in our charitable giving. Mom spent her last two months in their care, and there is no way for my family to repay the immense debt we owe the wonderful folks who work there. We hope that our gift will help other families in their time of need the same way that we benefited from those who supported the hospice before our introduction.

Consider Segregated Funds and Insurance Transfers

For money held in non-registered accounts, segregated funds and life insurance provide for quick and easy transfer of assets outside the will (avoiding delays and probate), sometimes in a matter of days. This can be an important advantage, both for transfers to family and, increasingly, for charitable gifts at death, thanks to recent CRA rule changes. However, these investments may not be for everyone, and care and consideration are needed when using them for these purposes.

Settling an estate that holds other non-registered investments can take significantly longer due to probate and other aspects in the settlement of the estate. If you do choose to use segregated funds and/or insurance for efficiency, it is important to ensure that you coordinate your will with your beneficiary designations on these products to ensure everything gets to where you want it to go.

In Mom's case, everything went smoothly, but I recently worked with a new client and discovered that her lawyer and stockbroker had not given coordinated instructions for the will and beneficiary designations of her segregated fund. The stockbroker had bypassed the client's will through the use of segregated fund beneficiaries, naming her son directly as full beneficiary of the proceeds. This would have led to a major problem in disbursing the estate had we not caught it in time. The will assumed that nearly $1,500,000 of her assets would transfer into the estate to fund a trust for her disabled son and provide for a large charitable bequest. Because the stockbroker had named her disabled son directly as a beneficiary, the result was going to be a huge increase in her taxes payable at death (as the charitable bequest would not have happened), and her son being removed from his Ontario Disability Support Program, as he would have inherited far more money than the program allowed.

Fortunately, when this client transferred her assets to us, we were able to correct this for her long before it became a problem. It could have been a disaster had we not made the discovery during our planning work.

Beware of Gifts of Set Amounts to Beneficiaries

One of the things that was super important to Mom was travel, so much so that she actually had a clause in her will that left money to my sister and me expressly for that purpose. When she last did her will, about eight years before she died, she set aside a modest amount that seemed reasonable. In that time period, however, both my sister and I had children, and the cost of travel increased substantially.

My mother was very concerned in her last days that the amount she had originally stated would not be enough to allow our whole families to travel, and she fixated on this, making Dad promise her daily that he would gift some extra funds to us to ensure we could take the whole family on a trip. Although neither my sister nor I were too concerned, it truly became a major concern to Mom, as she saw this as an important way for her to pass on one of her true passions in life to her kids and grandkids as part of her legacy.

I often suggest to clients that they talk to their lawyer about percentages and shares in their will rather than fixed amounts. As a financial planner, my concern is that you may not have enough funds in your estate at the end to meet set dollar figures, and that can impact cash flow for your survivors. In this case, though, the real risk was that the set amount was eroded by inflation, and the estate had more than enough to cover the true cost.

By the time Mom wanted to make changes, her mental capacity was in serious question and she was not able to revise her will legally. Dad had no issues honouring her wish using his own funds to make up the difference, but it is easy to see how under different circumstances a similar issue could end up with a will being contested by a beneficiary.

This is a tricky legal area. There are significant legal ramifications to naming flat-amount gifts in your will rather than a share or residual interest, and you should always have this conversation with your estate lawyer. A good estate lawyer can draft your will to address your concerns and ensure your wishes are followed in most circumstances.

Moving On, But Not Forgetting

I think it's fair to say that we are moving on as a family, but the best analogy I can give is that we feel like a person who has lost a limb; we adapt, but without Mom's presence we certainly aren't all that we used to be. All major life events have something to teach us, and the lessons learned in losing someone you love are perhaps the hardest of all; however, what we have learned has enriched our lives tremendously, and what we have lost we will continue to miss forever.

31

Back-Country Camping, Procrastination, and Planning

Our family are avid hikers and campers.[40] One of our finest back-country trips was when we went to the north end of Killarney Provincial Park and spent seven days travelling by canoe through the Grace Lake and Nellie Lake Loop. If you have never heard of it, Killarney was created by the efforts of the Group of Seven, and much of their most iconic work was painted in this area of the park.

We travelled with our good friends, who are the astronomer and artist in residence at the park, respectively, and very experienced back-country folk. This trip required a lot of up-front work

---

40 OK, I'll admit I lied: Bridget and I are. The boys, not so much. But we convince ourselves that they really secretly love it.

to ensure everyone's safety, to make sure it came off without a hitch, and to make it pay off for all of us in wonder and enjoyment. Little did I know that organizing a back-country camping trip would have so many similarities with my own financial planning practice! The same kinds of issues and skill sets come into play, and I'd like to share some of what we learned from camping experts on this trip that can be applied to financial and estate planning.

My hope is that you'll find this analogy motivating and that associating a fun camping holiday with financial planning might help you to stop procrastinating and start doing a lot more estate planning. One statistic I love to quote is that a bank study a number of years ago showed that only 20 percent of us "get off our butts" to make changes to our estate plans, or even to tackle them in the first place. I'd hazard a guess that no back-country hiker or canoeist would go out without a lot of planning.[41]

Start Planning Early While It's Cheap and Easy

As I said, our friends are expert back-country folk, which made our trip smoother and better organized than it would have been without all their planning. For starters, they knew a few quirks of the Ontario Parks reservation system that ensured we got back-country sites before most people even knew you could register. Not only did we get our pick of the prime, beautiful sites,

---

41 A back-country trip without planning means you will likely go out in a completely different, and terminal, kind of way.

but the costs of the trip might even have been higher if we had waited, as we would have had fewer options for travel available to us. With a very small number of camping sites available on each lake (usually only three or four), it can be insanely difficult to find a route that is canoeable within a reasonable timeframe. If a lake is booked, you either have to stay longer at another location, or skip it all together. Either option would have been more costly, and possibly made the whole trip impractical.

Estate planning works the same way: the sooner you start, the more options you have and the cheaper they are. For example, I've had many clients realize they need insurance at too late an age, only to discover that costs have become prohibitive. Or, that a non-existent or poorly written will may lead to your estate owing thousands of dollars in legal fees.

Additionally, many strategies designed to minimize your long-term taxation can require several years to execute. The younger you begin your planning, the less likely you will end up in a situation where your estate will be subject to a surprisingly high level of taxation. Almost always, getting a jump-start in your late forties or early fifties is a huge advantage over leaving things until you are sixty or seventy. Wait too long with financial and estate planning, and you will find it's an expensive mistake almost every time.

Pay for Quality Now; Save Hassle Later

One of our portage routes is known as "The Notch," and it's the steepest portage in the park. We had a forty-nine-pound Kevlar canoe large enough to carry the five of us, and we would have to carry it over the portage. It wasn't the cheapest canoe but, given that part of this portage is near-vertical, we were grateful we had spent the money on it rather than opting for the seventy-pound option that was half the price. Our friends warned us that they had originally bought a heavier canoe, came to regret it, and had to buy a second, lighter canoe. They lost a lot of money when selling the first canoe, regretting that they did not buy the right tool for the job the first time.

Cheaper doesn't always mean better in financial and estate planning, either. The choices you make usually involve a trade-off between long-term costs and short-term costs. Smart people start with what they need for the long term, rather than finding the cheapest option now that might cost way more later. One of the best examples of this is people who do a holograph will (hand-written) or use a "will kit" on their own, without visiting a lawyer. While it can be tempting to save money in the short term, in my experience, a huge percentage of wills done in this fashion end up being contested in court. One quirk of our system here in the province of Ontario is that if someone challenges your will, your estate will most likely be on the hook for all the legal costs, provided that a court deems the challenge to be reasonable. Such a challenge can easily end up costing five figures and can needlessly delay the disbursement of the estate. Don't skimp out — a few hundred dollars spent on a qualified estate lawyer now may save your heirs tens of thousands later.

Plan in Detail, Plan for the Unexpected, and Adjust the Plan as You Go

We meticulously worked out our Killarney trip schedule. Because we were in one of the most remote areas of the wilderness, we needed to detail in advance all the food and gear we would need, including planning for the unexpected along the way. When you head out into the back country, there's no going back once you get started. A bit of extra food, backup first-aid supplies, and other necessities are all smart choices. At one point near the end of our trip, I badly burned my hand on our camp stove. We had not thought to bring instant cold packs to deal with burns — but fortunately our friends, the more experienced campers, had. Trust me, they are now part of our regular kit.

Likewise, where your finances are concerned, a lot can happen to your financial life over the years and there is no going back to redo your plans and decisions. The best strategy is to put a plan in place early, try to anticipate possible downturns and challenging situations at the outset, and adjust as needed along the way to allow for changing circumstances. You will be better off in the long run. Studies show that people who have worked with a financial planner end up with asset values as much as 290 percent higher than those who don't.[42]

Hire someone with expertise. They have most likely seen more plans fail in their professional career than you can imagine exist,

---

42   According to the 2012 study *An Economic Analysis of Value of Advice in Canada* by Claude Montmarquette (CIRANO). See? Paying for planning work has a pretty big return on investment.

so you are paying to benefit from their knowledge. Failure is the best learning experience — provided that it's not your own failure you are learning from!

Get Insurance: It's Cheaper than the Alternatives

Our friend Bill—the astronomer in our power-camping couple—rents a special transponder for back-country hiking and canoeing, which includes an insurance plan if anyone is hurt on the trip. An air rescue from a remote area can run in the range of $10,000 to $20,000, and you don't want your life to be in danger or to be on the hook for that kind of money to get to safety.

If you are insurable and a reasonable age, the rate of return on an insurance policy for your estate is often hard to beat, compared with your potential ROI on investments on a risk-adjusted basis. This is particularly true for charitable gifts and for tax-planning purposes. I often find that people are most interested in insurance shortly after their health has taken a turn for the worse in some way. However, no insurance company is willing to take on someone with a recent diagnosis or issue, and it can often be months or years until you might become eligible for coverage again. Far better to do this while healthy and in advance of your later years. On holidays and in life, the point of any insurance is to cover you for catastrophic loss — if the worst happens.[43]

---

43 You might think death is the worst thing that can happen to you, but in many cases, there is actually a lot more financial strain on the family if you end up injured or sick. Don't overlook disability and critical illness insurance!

Be Prepared for Things that Can Throw You Off Course

The summer of our Killarney trip, Northern Ontario had a miserable year for bugs. We had spray and bug nets to keep the annoying things from driving us crazy and to prevent them from distracting us in their pesky way. Even so, in the course of our trip we met the largest beetle any of us had ever seen, and it hung around for an hour.

Your finances will have bugs, too — you can't plan for everything. Stuff will happen along the way, and that's why it's important to save and plan now, so we have capacity to be blown a bit off course with all the things we can't envision right now. We rarely make it all the way through life without a health crisis or financial crisis of some kind. In fact, most people probably face this at least once a decade. Doing some financial planning work now and putting funds aside in anticipation of an emergency is a very smart move. You know the old saying, "The Lord helps those who help themselves"? That should be your motto. Everyone should be putting money away into an emergency reserve to help cover the costs of all the annoying, pesky things life throws at us that we can't think of in advance.

Map Out Your Financial Picture

If you have been putting off tackling the details of your estate or financial planning, maybe it is time to start mapping out your journey. Without a clear plan for your financial future, you may never get to where you want to be, and you could get terribly lost in dangerous territory. Your lawyer, accountant, financial planner, and other professionals can help you create a clear path to follow to achieve your goals and minimize the pitfalls along the way. There's no time like the present, and nothing like a little expert advice, to begin planning for a smooth and rewarding trip through life.

32

The Charitable Gifts in My Own Estate

July is a special month in my family: Bridget and I celebrate our wedding anniversary, and both of my parents and I have birthdays. It is a busy month on the home front, for sure! Because I am a financial planning geek, we celebrated last July in my house by tweaking a few things in our estate plan.[44]

Recently, Bridget and I set up a second-to-die life insurance policy, which will pay out $250,000 upon the death of the second of us, as that is when the bulk of tax comes due in most couples' estates. Rather than naming our kids as the beneficiaries, we are going to make the beneficiaries our chosen charities.

This strategy will ultimately save our combined estate

---

44 It was incredibly exciting. As you no doubt suspect by now, I lead a wild and crazy life!

approximately $125,000 in income tax (based on today's tax rules) because the charities will each issue the estate a tax receipt for the amount received from the insurance. In most of the country, a $250,000 gift to charity made this way will save your estate approximately 50 percent in income tax.[45]

Who Gets the Cash?

In our case, there will be six charities each receiving a portion of those funds. Two of these charities (Amabile Choirs of London and the London Clay Art Centre) are local arts organizations my wife has belonged to, and which she loves dearly. Both have provided her with many friendships, much-needed stress relief from her job as a primary school teacher, and lifelong memories.

For my part, I've chosen two organizations as well, to which I have made long-standing volunteer commitments: The Secrets of Radar Museum, which I co-founded, and the Brain Tumour Foundation of Canada, for which I have volunteered for over a decade.

The last two organizations we chose, St. Joseph's Hospice and the Canadian Cancer Society, are newer additions to our list. We were extremely grateful to both organizations for the outstanding support our family received while my mom was dying, and we wanted to recognize that with our charitable giving.

---

45 The amount can range from approximately 40 percent to a high of 57 percent, depending on your province of residence and amount of income at death. Fifty percent is a reasonably accurate and simple proxy to use as an estimate.

Why Are We Doing It This Way?

For us, a gift of life insurance makes sense for a few reasons:

- It's cost-effective: For a couple between the ages of forty and seventy, an insurance strategy is very cost-effective relative to other gifts.

- It's fast: Unlike gifts of money made via bequest through the will, the organizations will get their funds within a couple of weeks. This also has the added benefit of bypassing the provincial probate process and greatly simplifying the estate's administration.

- It keeps our estate simpler: We have some complexities in our estate, and this keeps the charitable-giving part simple and clean.

- We can change our minds easily and with no cost: All it takes to tweak is an updating of the named beneficiaries.

- It sends a message to our kids about what is important to us.

How About You?

About 84 percent of Canadians give to charity each year, according to Statistics Canada, but less than 10 percent of us have thought about leaving something when we die to the charities and causes we value. There are a lot of creative ways to save tax on your estate, but this particular strategy has enormous benefits to the charities you leave the money to, and to the people and causes they support with their funds and services.

One of the beautiful aspects of insurance is that it allows those with even modest incomes to leave a fairly significant — and potentially transformational gift — to a charity at their death. What a wonderful way to align your estate plan with your values, minimize the tax impact on your estate, and leave a truly meaningful legacy that extends beyond your family and just keeps on giving. Bridget and I are pretty excited about making a legacy of transformational gifts when we are gone.[46] Why not talk to your lawyer or advisor about how you can do something similar?

---

46 Well, maybe not so excited about the "when we are gone" part, but more so about the transformational gift part! As happy as we are to make the gift, we're in no rush for it to happen.

Epilogue

Our Most Important Legacy

For Bridget and me, legacy has a deeper meaning than just our wealth, or even to whom or to what causes we donate through our estate. To us, money is ultimately just a tool that we use to engage in the world around us, and it has no intrinsic value of its own. So, for us, our legacy is the way in which we touch the world and the people around us and the footprints that we will leave behind. We hope that we are leading our lives in such a way that our children, grandchildren, and all of our descendants will be proud to know that they are related to us.

From a very young age, we have worked hard to try and pass these values down to our children, and we feel that it is important to provide as much leadership by example as we can. We each have been shaped by the values that were passed down to us by our parents and by some special times in our lives that became defining, seminal moments for how we approach our lives and the raising of our children.

In my own life, one of those moments was at the tender age of six, when Terry Fox ran a section of his daily Marathon of Hope just a few kilometres from the very small town in which I grew up. As children, our lives revolve around ourselves and our own needs, but something changed that day. As Terry ran nearby, we talked in school about what he was doing, and I went home and watched the news. I was amazed that another kid — a young man with only one leg — was engaged in something as big and incredible as his cross-country run for cancer. For the first time, my awareness of the world unfolded well beyond my own sense of self. That moment changed my life in a way that still affects me today.

When our oldest son was four, we had him clean out his old toys, and together we brought them down to a local women's shelter where he proudly donated them to the kids. A couple of years later, just before he turned six, after hearing the news about the houses destroyed in the Haiti earthquake, he turned to us with tears in his eyes and asked us, "Would it be OK to have my friends bring money to help people rebuild houses instead of presents for my birthday this year?" A few weeks later, he walked into Habitat for Humanity (our chosen charity to send funds to Haiti) with a baggie containing $280.

It still makes me misty-eyed to think about that day. I realize that, for him, the Haiti earthquake will be his own "Terry Fox" moment, and I think it is poetic that for both of us such a key moment would come at the age of six. Today he is a teenager, and that big heart remains; he is dedicated to seeing the world be a better place than it was the day before.

Each of our three boys has had their own moment when they have engaged with the world on a different level. By no means are our children perfect,[47] but we are proud that our value system has been passed on to them, and of how they, in turn, have encouraged us to become better humans as well.

Increasingly, I feel that our society's pursuit of wealth for wealth's sake alone, along with overwhelming pressures to consume in the name of self-gratification have taken something very important from our humanity. In an era in which civility, patience, and tolerance seem to be increasingly hard to find in the wider world, I can't help but think that we each need to think about how our actions and our personal values can and should positively impact the people and world around us. This may be the most important legacy question of all, and in many ways, it has nothing to do with money.

I'm immensely proud of the professional work I have done and the amazing folks we have been blessed to call clients, friends, and

---

47 At least once a week, we contemplate selling at least one of our children to the circus. If you have children (especially all boys!), I know you've had days like this too, so don't judge us too harshly . . .

partners over the years. At the time of writing this book, our firm has been involved in almost $30,000,000 in charitable gifts in the last six years (that we know of). I suspect the true number may be vastly higher, as we don't always know the final outcome of some of the educational work that we do on behalf of the charities who hire us to talk to their donors. All the generous clients we have helped with their bequests and planned giving are leveraging their wealth to leave a bigger legacy; the money they donate through their estate plans is a tool to help them help others, thereby leaving the world a better place. Driven by purpose, they are making their mark on the future by making a difference where there is need.

If you are in our neighbourhood, give us a call, or visit our website at www.drivenbypurpose.ca for tools and resources to help you own your legacy.

About the Author

R yan Fraser is a nationally known expert in financial planning and philanthropy, with an extensive background as a leader, volunteer, and founder of many charitable organizations. After fifteen years in management positions in the financial industry, Ryan founded his firm, Quiet Legacy Planning Group Ltd., which specializes in working with individuals who wish to incorporate their personal value system into their financial planning experience.

Ryan is a faculty member for the Master Financial Advisor – Philanthropy Designation (MFA-P™), as well as the Canadian Association of Gift Planner's Gift Planning Fundamentals course. He is a past president of the Estate Planners Council of London as well as a past chair of the Canadian Association of Gift Planners London Roundtable. He was founding president of The

Secrets of Radar Museum and has served extensively in leadership positions on boards and committees of numerous not-for-profit organizations, including Brain Tumour Foundation of Canada, London Heritage Council, Trillium Plus Music & Letters and many others.

Ryan's extensive commitment to the not-for-profit sector has been twice recognized by the Province of Ontario, which awarded him the Ontario Volunteer Service Award in both 2009 and 2015. He is a graduate of both the University of Michigan and the University of Western Ontario, where he was awarded the University Gold Medal.

Beyond his passion for philanthropy and finance, he is also an award-winning astrophotographer whose works have been featured by Canada's national astronomy magazine *SkyNews*, and across Canada on CTV. Ryan's wife Bridget and their three children, Brennan, Liam, and Haydn, are his inspiration for philanthropy and community service.

CPSIA information can be obtained
at www.ICGtesting.com
Printed in the USA
LVHW021950240121
677375LV00029B/1399

9 781988 344225